G000139241

THE EDEXCEL POETRY ANTHOLOGY: RELATIONSHIPS – THE STUDENT GUIDE

DAVID WHEELER

Red Axe Books

ISBN: 978-1911477310

© David Wheeler

Find us at:

www.dogstailbooks.co.uk

CONTENTS

Introduction

I hope you find this revision guide useful. It consists of an individual analysis of each poem in The Edexcel Anthology – Relationships. The analysis of each poem follows the same pattern: there is a section on the poet and the context in which the poem was written and some facts about each author; unfamiliar words are explained; and then each poem has a commentary which focuses on both what the poem is about and the style, form and structure that the poet uses. A final section on each poem summarizes the poem's overall impact and effect. There are no colours, few illustrations, but you will get a clear sense of what each poem is about and each poem's overall effect.

Who or what is this book for?

Perhaps you missed that crucial lesson on one particular poem that you find hard to understand? Good lessons are better than this book, because through different activities and through careful questioning and probing your teacher will help you to arrive at an understanding, an appreciation of the poem that you work out for yourself – and that process is invaluable – it's a process of thinking and exploring as a group, in a pair perhaps and as an individual, and, no matter how good the notes that your class-mates made, those notes are no substitute for having been there and gone through the process of the lesson. So, maybe, through absence, you feel a little out of touch with some of the poems: this book will help you.

Alternatively, you may want to read about ideas which you have not encountered in class. Alternatively, you may have the sort of teacher who allows you to respond in your own way to the poems; that is a completely valid and worthwhile approach, of course, but it does not suit every student: some students like to have clear guidelines about the meaning of what they read and to have various interpretations suggested to them so that they are at least aware of the overall gist of the poem. It still leaves you free to make up your own mind and have your own ideas, but it does provide a starting point – this book will give you that starting point.

You may be trying to revise the poems in the final days and weeks before the exam and want a quick refresher on poems that you first studied in class a long time ago; maybe it was a Friday afternoon and you weren't paying complete attention; maybe you were late for the lesson and never quite 'got' what the poem is about; maybe you were distracted by something more interesting happening outside and spent the lesson gazing out of the window. This book will help you get to grips with those poems.

It is very unlikely, but you may be reading these poems on your own for the very first time – this book will help you too, because I have assumed that you know nothing about the poem or about poetry, and the commentary on each poem is written so that you can start from scratch. Of course, some of you might find this a tiny bit condescending – and I apologize for that. I should also apologize if there are ideas in this book which are different from ones you have encountered before in class. There are as many different ways to read a poem as there are readers, and each reader might have a slightly different view of a particular poem – as we shall see. For example, most readers (pupils, teachers, professional critics) would agree that 'London' by William Blake is critical of the society he lived in; most would agree that 'London' is a bitter attack on the London that he lived in, but quite what the final verse means is open to a variety of interpretations!

So... if you want a book that tells you what each poem means; comments on features of style and structure; suggests the tone or the overall impact of each poem; gives you the necessary background knowledge to understand each poem – then this is it. At the end you will find a glossary of poetic terms, but after this introduction, there is a commentary on each poem – each commentary is self-contained and can be read on its own. Throughout the book I have used the words that I would use if I were teaching a lesson on these poems – if I use words you don't know or haven't heard, then look them up. Part of education, part of writing well about Literature is the way you yourself write, so to expand your vocabulary is a good thing. Terms which have specific literary meanings are all in the glossary at the back of the book.

Help Yourself!

I hope you find this book helpful in some ways, perhaps many ways. It deliberately does not include very detailed information about the authors for two reasons. Firstly, it would be a waste of space. Secondly, the internet is a rich source of information about writers and their work – an internet search on any of your studied poets or poems will throw up all sorts of interesting resources, including student chat boards, online revision chat-rooms as well as more obvious sources of information like Wikipedia or web sites associated with a particular author. Where there is detailed biographical information here, it is because it is vital to an understanding of the poem.

But do be warned – all the information you can possibly find about a particular poet may help to clarify something you already sensed about the poem, but it is no substitute for engagement with the poem itself. And in the examination the examiner does not want to read a potted biography of the poet whose poem you have chosen to write about. Besides - generalizing from what we know about a writer or his/her era is a dangerous thing: for example, it is important to be aware of William Blake's political beliefs and to be aware that he wrote 'London' during the years of the French Revolution – some might say that without such an awareness the poem cannot be fully appreciated and understood – BUT that will not help you explain the impact of individual words and lines and images at all, nor will it help you write well in the examination. Very often I have started my commentary on a poem with necessary information to help you understand it, but you don't need to reproduce all that information in the exam - it is there to help you fully understand significant details about the poem; to try to reproduce the process of discovery that a good lesson will guide you through. But it probably has little place in the examination.

You may be the sort of student who is doing English Language or English Literature because it is compulsory at your school. But it may also be that as you progress through the course you come to feel that English is a subject that you like and are good at; you may even be intrigued or fascinated by some of the poems in the anthology. If that happens, then do not rely on this book. Look on the internet for resources that will further your interest. For example, if one poet makes a special impact on you – read some of their other work; you will find a lot of it available on-line. Many of the poets in the Literary Heritage sections are now out of copyright – their work is freely available on-line. Many of the contemporary poets have their own websites which can be a fascinating source of extra information and contain links to other poems or biographical information. So there are many ways in which you can help yourself: it's a good habit to get into, especially if you start thinking about the possibility of doing English at A level.

But please remember this is no substitute for a close engagement with the poems themselves. And just as importantly – this book is no substitute for a good lesson which allows you to think about the poem's language and ideas, and then slowly come to an understanding of it. After understanding it (and that is an emotional as much as a logical understanding of it), you may come to appreciate it. What does that mean? Well, as you go through the course and read more and more poems then you may find that you prefer some to others. The next step is to identify why you prefer some poems to others: in this there are no right answers, but there are answers which are clearer and better expressed than others. And preference must be based on reasons to do with the way the poem is written or its overall emotional impact: it's your job to put what you think and feel into words – I cannot help you do that. I can merely point out some of the important features and meanings of the poems. As you grow in confidence and perhaps read other writing on these poems or listening to your teacher or your classmates, then you will start to formulate your own opinions – stealing an idea from one person, a thought from somewhere else and combining all these different things into your own view of the poem. And that is appreciation. As soon as you say you prefer one poem to another you are engaging in a critical reaction to what you have read – in exactly the same way that people prefer one film to another or one song or performer to another.

Romanticism

In this cluster of poems the first three are designated Romantic poems and it is important that you have an understanding of what Romanticism was. It has very little to do with the word 'romantic' as we apply it today to an event like Valentine's Day.

Romanticism is the name given to the artistic, political and cultural movement that emerged in England and Germany in the 1790s and in the rest of Europe in the 1820s and beyond. It was a movement that saw great changes in literature, painting, sculpture, architecture and music, and found its catalyst in the new philosophical ideas of Jean Jacques Rousseau and Thomas Paine, and in response to the American, French and industrial revolutions. Its chief emphasis was on freedom of individual self-expression, sincerity, spontaneity and originality, but it also looked to the distant past of the Middle Ages for some of its inspiration. In Romantic thought the nature of the poet changed: no longer was a poet someone who could manipulate words well and with skill; the poet was a special individual with a unique vision to communicate and with special insights to communicate through his poetry.

The key characteristics of Romantic poetry in English are:

- a reverence for and veneration of the natural world.
- a belief that the poet was a special person who had important truths to communicate and whose experiences were more intense than those of ordinary people.
- an emphasis on individualism and intense emotion.

- an increased interest in ordinary people – the rural poor and the urban working classes.
- a political radicalism, best summed up by the watchwords of the French Revolution – liberty, fraternity, equality.
- an overwhelming emphasis on the sensibility and imagination of the poet.
- an interest in medieval and ancient history.
- a veneration of Shakespeare.
- a desire to be original and to reject the orthodoxies of the immediate past.

Of course, not all the poets that we label 'Romantic' displayed all these characteristics all through their careers.

Contemporary Poetry & the Literary Heritage

You will probably have noticed that the poems within each section or cluster of your anthology are designated as Literary Heritage poems. Why? Contemporary poetry consists of poems written in the very recent past by living poets and they are here because as you study English or English Literature, it is felt to be important that you realize that poetry is not dead and poetry is not only written by dead white Englishmen: it is alive and it is being written now all over the English-speaking world by men and by women from a wide variety of backgrounds. So the contemporary poems are there to remind you that poetry is alive and well and thriving. Indeed, as I have already mentioned, many of the contemporary poets have their own websites or perform poetry readings which you may be lucky enough to attend during your course. You can also see some performances of these poems on the internet.

The poems in the first half of the anthology are generally by dead white Englishmen, although there are some poems by women. That sounds dismissive (dead white Englishmen), but it's not meant to be. They are in the anthology to remind you that writers have been writing poetry in English for hundreds of years and that what happens over those centuries is that an agreement emerges about which poems are some of the greatest or most significant ever written in the English Language. How does such agreement emerge? Well, mainly through people continuing to read the poems, responding to them and enjoying them; another concrete way is for the poems to appear in anthologies – which ensures them an even wider audience. The point you need to grasp is that writing in English poetry has been going on for hundreds of years and what has been written in the past influences what is written now. Many contemporary poets will have read the poems that you will read in the Literary Heritage sections. So when you read, for example, 'Love's Philosophy' by Percy Shelley for the first time, you will be joining the millions of English-speaking people all over the world who have read and enjoyed that sonnet. Organizations like the BBC have also run public votes where members of the public can vote for their favourite poem – another way that we know which poems are popular. Such poems then become part of the canon such as those by Robert Browning and his wife, Elizabeth Barrett Browning That is not to say, however, that there is only agreement about the value of poems from the distant past: some like those by Charles Causley and Seamus Heaney are from the closing decades of the 20th century; they are included because already there is widespread agreement that these poets are important and influential and that their poems are rewarding to read and study and enjoy.

So part of our heritage, part of the culture of speaking English, whether you speak English in Delhi or London or Manchester or Lahore or Trinidad or Liverpool or Auckland or Toronto or Cape Town or Chicago, is centuries of English poetry and a continuing poetic culture which is rich and vibrant, and includes voices from all over the English-speaking world.

The Secret of Poetry

The secret of poetry, of course, is that there is no secret. Nonetheless, I have come across lots of students who find poetry challenging or off-putting or who don't like it for some reason. I find this attitude bizarre for all sorts of reasons. But some students are very wary of poetry or turned off by it. If you are – rest assured: you shouldn't be!

Poetry is all around us: in proverbial sayings, in popular music, in the nursery rhymes we listen to or sing as children, in playground skipping chants, even in the chanting heard at football matches. All these things use the basic elements of poetry: rhythm and rhyming and very often the techniques of poetry – alliteration, repetition, word play. Advertisements and newspaper headlines also use these techniques to make what they say memorable. Ordinary everyday speech is full of poetry: if you say that something is 'as cheap as chips' you are using alliteration and a simile; if you think someone is 'two sandwiches short of a picnic', if someone is 'a pain in the arse', then you are using metaphors – the only difference is that when poets use similes and metaphors they try to use ones that are fresh and original – and memorable, in the same away that a nursery rhyme or your favourite song lyrics are memorable. Even brand names or shop names use some of the techniques of poetry: if you have a Kwik Fit exhaust supplier in your town you should note the word-play (the mis-spelling of Kwik) and the assonance – the repetition of the 'i' sound. There must be several hundred ladies' hairdressers in the UK called 'Curl Up and Dye' – which is comic word-play. You may go to 'Fat Face' because you like what they sell, but I hope that when you go next time, you'll spare a thought for the alliteration and assonance in the shop's name.

Poets also play with words. So when students tell me they don't like poetry, I don't believe them – I feel they have simply not approached it in the right way. Or perhaps not seen the link between the poetry of everyday life and the poetry they have to study and analyze for GCSE.

Poetry has been around a very long time: the earliest surviving literature in Europe consists of poetry. As far as we can tell poetry existed even before writing, and so poems were passed down by word of mouth for centuries before anyone bothered to write them down. If something is going to be passed down and remembered in this way, then it has to be memorable. And, as we shall see, poets use various techniques and tricks and patterns to make what they write easy to remember or striking in some way - just as you may remember the words to your favourite song or to a nursery rhyme that was recited to you as a small child. Let us take one example. The opening sentence of Charles Dickens' novel *A Tale of Two Cities* is

It was the best of times; it was the worst of times.

It is not poetry, but it is very memorable, because Dickens uses simple repetition, parallelism and paradox to create a very memorable sentence. Parallelism because the two halves of the sentence are the same – except for one word; and paradox because the two words – best and worst – seem to contradict each other. Now look at this recent slogan from an advert for Jaguar cars:

Don't dream it. Drive it.

This uses the same techniques as Dickens: parallelism and paradox (or juxtaposition) and it also uses alliteration. It is all about manipulating words to give them greater impact – to make them memorable.

As I am sure I will repeat elsewhere, it is always vital to read a poem aloud: your teacher might do it very well, you might be lucky enough to hear one of the living poets in the anthology read their poems aloud or you can access many recordings via the internet. I think reading a poem aloud is a good way to revise it: it has been claimed that when we read something aloud we are reading twenty times slower than when we read with our eyes – and that slowness is vital, because it allows the sound of the poem, the turn of each phrase and the rhythm of each poem to stand out. As we shall see, the way a poem sounds is absolutely crucial to its impact – for one thing, it helps you pick out techniques such as alliteration and assonance.

One of the things we will discover is that poetry is partly about pattern – patterns of sounds, of words, of rhythm; patterns of lay-out too, so that a poem and the way it is set out on the page - often separated into separate stanzas (don't call them verses) – is vital. If you quickly glance at a page from the anthology, you would probably assume that what is on the page is a poem – because we have certain expectations of the way that poems look. So what? You have probably been aware for a long time that poets often organize what they write into stanzas. For me this is an absolutely crucial part of poetry because as human beings we are in love with patterns, we are addicted to patterns – and that is one of the many reasons we love poetry or find it so appealing. Patterns dominate our lives. We may have patterns on our clothes, our furnishings, our curtains, our carpets. But patterns rule our lives more completely than that: seen from above even a housing estate has patterns – the street lights at regular intervals, the garages and gardens in the same relationship to the houses; a spider's web on a frosty morning; the unique patterns of snowflakes; a honeycomb; your school uniform perhaps; the rhythm of your day, of the timetable you follow at school, of your week, of the seasons and of the year. And where patterns do not exist we like to invent them: the periodic table of elements (which you may be familiar with from Chemistry) does not exist as a table out there in nature – it's the human need to organize and give things a pattern which is responsible for the way it looks. Or look at a map of the world, criss-crossed by lines of longitude and latitude – and invented by the human mind as an aid for navigation.

What on earth has this to do with poetry? Well, poetry, especially from the past, likes to follow patterns and this structure that poets choose is something we instinctively like; it is also important when poets set up a pattern, only to break it to make whatever they are saying even more memorable because it breaks the pattern. We will see this happen in some of the poems in the anthology.

Let us look at it another way. Take the sonnet: if you choose to write a sonnet, you are committing yourself to trying to say what you want to say in 140 syllables, arranged in equal lines of 10 syllables each and fitted to a complex rhyming scheme. It is very hard to do, so why bother?

Partly because it is a challenge – to force you to condense what you want to say into 140 syllables concentrates the mind and, more importantly, makes for language that can be very condensed and full of meaning. And, of course, the sonnet has been around for centuries so to choose to write one now means you are following (and hoping to bring something new and surprising) to a long-established form.

So what is poetry? *The Oxford Concise Dictionary of Literary Terms* defines it as:

Language sung, chanted, spoken, or written according to some pattern of recurrence that emphasizes the relationships between words on the basis of sound as well as sense: this pattern is almost always a rhythm or metre, which may be supplemented by rhyme or alliteration or both. All cultures have their poetry, using it for various purposes from sacred ritual to obscene insult, but it is generally employed in those utterances and writings that call for heightened intensity of emotion, dignity of expression, or subtlety of meditation. Poetry is valued for combining pleasures of sound with freshness of ideas....

Remember some of these phrases as you read this book or as you read the poems in the Anthology – which poems have intensity of emotion? Are there some which have a freshness of ideas? Or do some make you think about things more deeply (subtlety of meditation)? Perhaps there are poems which make you do all three? What can I possibly add to the Oxford Book of Literary Terms? Think of your favourite song – whatever type of music you listen to. The song's lyrics will share many of the characteristics of poetry, but the words will be enhanced by the music and the delivery of the vocalist. Is it a song that makes you happy or sad? Angry or mellow? Whatever it makes you feel, a song takes you on an emotional journey – and that is what poems do too, except they lack musical accompaniment. So think of a poem as being like a song – designed to make you feel a particular emotion and think particular thoughts; like some songs, the emotions, the thoughts, may be quiet complex and hard to explain but the similarity is there. And that is another reason why it is important to hear the poems read aloud – they are designed to be listened to, not simply read. Short poems like the ones in the Anthology are often called lyric poems – and that is because hundreds of years ago they would have been accompanied by music. Before 1066 Anglo-Saxon bards telling even long narrative poems used to accompany themselves on a lyre – a primitive type of guitar and up to Elizabethan times lyric poems were set to music and performed.

Making Connections

As you can see from what is written above, a lot of the work in English on the Anthology is about making connections – the exam question will explicitly ask you to do this. As you study the Anthology or read this book you should try to make connections for yourself. Free your mind and make unusual connections. You might feel that some poems take you on a similar emotional journey; some poems might use metaphor or personification in similar ways; some poems were written at the same time as others and are connected by their context.

If you can connect poems because of their written style or something like structure or technique, then that will impress the examiner more than if you simply connect them by subject matter. The poems are already connected by simply being in the Anthology, so to start an answer, for example, by stating that two poems are about 'Conflict' is a waste of words. You should try to do some thinking for yourself as you read this book and reflect on the poems in the anthology– because it is a good habit to get into and helps prepare you mentally for the exam.

Do you have a favourite word? If you do, you might like to think about why you like it so much. It may well have something to do with the meaning, but it might also have something to do with the sound. Of course, some words are clearly onomatopoeic like *smash*, *bang* and *crack*. But other words have sound qualities too which alter the way we react to them – and they are not obviously onomatopoeic. For example, the word *blister* sounds quite harsh because the letter *b* and the combination of *st* sound a little unpleasant; and, of course, we know what a *blister* is and it is not a pleasant thing. On the other hand, words like *fearful* or *gentle* or *lightly* have a lighter, more delicate sound because of the letters from which they are made. Words like *glitter* and *glisten* cannot be onomatopoeic: onomatopoeia is all about imitating the sound that something makes and *glitter* and *glisten* refer to visual phenomena, but the the *gl* at the start and the *st* and *tt* in the middle of the words make them sound entirely appropriate, just right, don't they?

Think of it another way: just reflect on the number of swear words or derogatory terms in English which start with *b* or *p*: *bloody, bugger, bastard, plonker, pratt, prick, prawn* – the list goes on and on. The hard *c* sound in a word like *cackle* is also unpleasant to the ear. So what? Well, as you read poems try to be aware of this, because poets often choose light, gentle sounds to create a gentle atmosphere: listen to the sounds. Of course, the meaning of the word is the dominant element that we respond to, but listen to it as well.

You don't need to know anything about the history of the English language to get a good grade at GCSE. However, where our language comes from makes English unique. English was not spoken in the British Isles until about 450 CE when tribes from what is now Holland invaded as the Roman Empire gradually collapsed. The language these tribes spoke is now known as Old English – if you were to see some it would look very foreign to your eyes, but it is where our basic vocabulary comes from. A survey once picked out the hundred words that are most used in written English: ninety-nine of them had their roots in Old English; the other one was derived from French. The French the Normans spoke had developed from Latin and so when we look at English vocabulary – all the words that are in the dictionary – we can make a simple distinction between words that come from Old English and words that come from Latin – either directly from Latin or from Latin through French. [I am ignoring for the moment all the hundreds of thousands of words English has adopted from all the other languages in the world.]

So what? I hear you think. Well, just as the sounds of words have different qualities, so do the words derived from Old English and from

Latin. Words that are Old English in origin are short, blunt and down-to-earth; words derived from Latin or from Latin through French are generally longer and sound more formal. Take a simple example: house, residence, domicile. *House* comes from Old English; *residence* from Latin through French and *domicile* direct from Latin. Of course, if you invited your friends round to your residence, they would probably think you were sounding rather fancy – but that is the whole point. We associate words of Latinate origin with formality and elegance and sometimes poets might use words conscious of the power and associations that they have. Where a poet has used largely Latinate vocabulary it creates a special effect and there are poems in the Anthology where I have pointed this feature out. Equally, the down to earth simplicity of words of English origin can be robust and strong.

Alliteration is a technique that is easy to recognize and is used by many poets and writers to foreground their work. It can exist, of course, in any language. However, it seems to have appealed to writers in English for many centuries. Before 1066 when the Normans invaded and introduced French customs and culture, poetry was widely written in a language we now call Old English, or Anglo Saxon. Old English poetry did not rhyme. How was it patterned then? Each line had roughly the same number of syllables, but what was more important was that each line had three or four words that alliterated. Alliterative poetry continued to be written in English until the 14th century and if you look at these phrases drawn from everyday English speech I think you can see that it has a power even today: busy as a bee, cool as a cucumber, good as gold, right as rain, cheap as chips, dead as a doornail, kith and kin, hearth and home, spick and span, hale and hearty. Alliteration can also be found in invented names. Shops: Coffee Corner, Sushi Station, Caribou Coffee, Circuit City. Fictional characters: Peter Pan, Severus Snape, Donald Duck, Mickey Mouse, Nicholas Nickleby, Humbert Humbert, King Kong, Peppa Pig. The titles of films and novels: *Pride and Prejudice, Sense and Sensibility, Debbie Does Dallas, House on Haunted Hill, Gilmour Girls, V for Vendetta, A Christmas Carol, As Good as it Gets, The Witches of Whitby,*

The Wolf of Wall Street. Alliteration is an easy way to make words and phrases memorable.

So what? Well, as you read the poems and see alliteration being used, I think it is helpful to bear in mind that alliteration is not some specialized poetic technique, but is part of the fabric of everyday English too and it is used in everyday English for the same reasons that it is used by poets – to make the words more memorable.

An Approach to Poetry

This next bit may only be relevant if you are studying the poems for the first time and it is an approach that I use in the classroom. It works well and helps students get their bearing when they first encounter a poem. These are the Five Ws. They are not my idea, but I use them in the classroom all the time. They are simply five questions which are a starting point, a way of getting into the poem and a method of approaching an understanding of it. With some poems some of the answers to the questions are more important than others; with some poems these questions and our answers to them will not get us very far at all – but it is where we will start. I will follow this model with each commentary. They are also a good way to approach the unseen poem. The five questions to ask of each poem you read are:

- Who?

- When?

- Where?

- What?

- Why?

WHO? Who is in the poem? Whose voice the poem uses? This is the first and most basic question. In many poems the poet speaks as themselves, but sometimes they are ventriloquists – they pretend to be someone else. So first of all we must identify the voice of the poem. We must ask ourselves to whom the poem is addressed. It isn't always right to say – the reader; some poems are addressed to a particular individual. And, of course, there may well be other people mentioned in the poem itself. Some poetry is quite cryptic, so who 'you' and 'they' are in a poem make a crucial difference to the way we interpret it. Why are poems 'cryptic'? Well, one reason is that they use language in a very compressed way – compressed perhaps because of the length of each line or the decision to use rhyme.

WHEN? When was the poem written and when is it set? This is where context is important. We know our context: we are reading the poem now, but when the poem was written and when the poem is set (not always the same, by any means) is crucial to the way we interpret it. The gender or background of the poet might be important, the society they were living in, the circumstances which led them to write the poem – all these things can be crucial to how we interpret the poem.

WHERE? Where is the poem set? Where do the events described in the poem take place? With some poems this question is irrelevant; with others it is absolutely vital – it all depends on the poem. In the Anthology you will find some poems which depend on some understanding of where they are set for them to work; you will find other poems where the location is not specified or is irrelevant or generalized – again it depends on the poem.

WHAT? This means what happens in a poem. Some poems describe a place; some describe a particular moment in time; some tell a story; some have a story buried beneath their surface; some make statements – some may do several or all of these things at once. They are all potentially different, but what happens is something very basic and should be grasped before you can move on to really appreciate a poem. Very often I have kept this section really short, because it is only when you start to look closely at language that you fully understand what is going on.

WHY? This is the hardest question of all and the one with a variety of possible answers, depending on your exact view of the poem in question. I like to think of it asking ourselves 'Why did the poet write this poem?' Or what is the overall message or emotional impact of this poem? To answer it with every poem, we need to look at all the other questions, the way the poet uses language and its effect on us, and try to put into words the tone of the voice of the poem and the poem's overall impact. Students in the classroom often seem puzzled by my asking them to discuss the poem's tone. But it boils down to this - if you were reading the poem out loud, what tone of voice would you use? What is the mood or atmosphere of the poem? Does the poet, or whoever the poet is pretending to be, have a particular attitude to what he or she is writing about? Answering these questions helps us discuss the tone of the poem. But you may not agree with everybody else about this and this is good: through disagreement and discussion, our understanding of what we read is sharpened. In the commentaries on each poem in this Anthology this question 'Why?' is answered at the very end of each commentary, because it is only after looking closely at the poet's use of language, form and structure that we can begin to answer it. If you feel you know the poem well enough, you might just use the section 'Why?' for each poem as a quick reminder of what its main message is. For all the poems the 'Why?' section consists of a series of bullet points which attempt to give you the words to express what the poem's main point is.

A Word of Warning

This book and the commentaries on individual poems that follow are full of words to do with literature – the technical devices such as metaphor, simile, oxymoron. These are the vocabulary to do with the craft of writing and it is important that you understand them and can use them with confidence. It is the same as using the word *osmosis* in Biology or *isosceles* in Maths. However, in the examination, it is absolutely pointless to pick out a technique unless you can write something vaguely intelligent about its effect – the effect is vital! The examiner will know when a poet is using alliteration and does not need you to point it out;

the sort of writing about poetry that consists of picking out technical devices and saying nothing about their effect or linking them in some meaningful way to the subject matter is worthless. I will suggest, in each commentary, what the effect might be, but we can generalize and say that all techniques with words are about making the poem memorable in some away – and this 'making something memorable' is also about foregrounding language. Language that is foregrounded means that it is different from normal everyday language and that it draws attention to itself by being different – it would be like if we all went round every day and tried to use a metaphor and alliteration in everything that we said or if we tried speaking in rhyme all day – people would notice!

Warming Up

Before we look at any of the poems from the anthology, I want to briefly examine some poems (which focus on relationships) to give you a taste of the approach that will be followed throughout the rest of the book. So we will start by looking at some completely different poems. I am going to subject all the poems to a full analysis, but I will demonstrate with the poems some crucial ways of reading poetry and give you some general guidance which will stand you in good stead when we deal with the poems in the anthology itself. This is not meant to confuse you, but to help. I cannot stress enough that these poems are not ones that you will be assessed on. They are my choice – and I would use the same method in the classroom – introducing a class very slowly to poetry and 'warming up' for the anthology by practising the sorts of reading skills which will help with any poem. Besides, you may find the method valuable in your preparation for answering on the unseen poem in the exam.

Here is the first poem we will consider – one of the most famous love poems in the English Language – Sonnet 116 by William Shakespeare:

SONNET 116

Let me not to the marriage of true minds
Admit impediments. Love is not love
Which alters when it alteration finds,
Or bends with the remover to remove:
O no; it is an ever-fixed mark,
That looks on tempests, and is never shaken;
It is the star to every wandering bark,
Whose worth's unknown, although his height be taken.
Love's not Time's fool, though rosy lips and cheeks
Within his bending sickle's compass come;
Love alters not with his brief hours and weeks,
But bears it out even to the edge of doom.
    If this be error and upon me proved,
    I never writ, nor no man ever loved.

Context

Shakespeare is the most famous writer England has ever produced and his plays are known throughout the world. 'Sonnet 116' by William Shakespeare is part of a sonnet sequence of 154 sonnets – also known as a sonnet cycle. Readers have commented that in the sonnets as a whole, Shakespeare covers every aspect of arguably the most important and strongest human emotion – love - as well as our most powerful instinct – sexual desire and the whole range of what happens in what we now call human relationships. Unlike Shakespeare's plays (most of which were unpublished during his lifetime), the sonnets were published in 1609. What does this tell us? We are not entirely sure: it is generally felt that it shows that poetry was held in higher regard than writing plays, so perhaps Shakespeare published the sonnets to achieve fame and wealth; there is also the fact that in Shakespeare's era there were no copyright laws – so once a play was published, there was nothing to stop any theatre putting a play on without giving the writer any performance fees.

Of the 154 sonnets some are very famous and appear in many anthologies. These very famous ones are well-known by the general public too: in the past, BBC Radio 4 has sometimes run public surveys to discover the nation's favourite poem or the nation's favourite love poem and Shakespeare's sonnets are frequently voted into the top ten. If you like 'Sonnet 116', then you might like to read some of his others. They are readily available on-line and are known by their number and the first line:

Sonnet 18 – Shall I compare thee to a summer's day?

Sonnet 29 – When in disgrace with Fortune and men's eyes

Sonnet 55 – Not marble or the gilded monuments

Sonnet 57 – Being your slave what should I do?

Sonnet 71 – No longer mourn for me when I am dead

Sonnet 91 – Some glory in their birth, some in their skill

Sonnet 129 – The expense of spirit in a waste of shame

Sonnet 130 – My mistress' eyes are nothing like the sun

Because so little is known about Shakespeare's private life, there has been endless speculation about who the sonnets are addressed to – but none of this speculation helps us get any closer to the individual sonnets and their meaning and impact. Personally I find it of no interest whatsoever, because for me the words are what make the sonnets memorable and worth reading now – over four hundred years since they were first published.

'Sonnet 116' is often used in modern marriage services (nowadays some churches allow couples considerable freedom in choosing some of the words they use during the service) and I have even seen cards for sale which reproduce the words of the sonnet – these cards are intended to be sent to people who are getting married. The whole sonnet presents a love that is steadfast and loyal and unchanging in the face of other changes. We will look closely at the language and tone of the sonnet, but also consider a deeper and darker interpretation.

impediments – obstacles.

or...remove – or ends when one person leaves or stops the relationship.

ever-fixèd – permanent, not moving.

bark – ship.

time's fool – the fool of time, subject to time and ageing.

bending sickle – a scythe and its curved shape; the Grim Reaper carries a sickle; sickles and scythes are long-handled tools used for chopping down tall crops or weeds; here it is used metaphorically – Time chops us down because we succumb to age and finally death.

compass – range.

bears it out – endures it.

doom – Doomsday, the end of the world in Christian mythology, the day of Final Judgement when Christ will come to earth again and decide who goes to Heaven and who to Hell. Shakespeare uses this to suggest that love will last forever – until the end of time or the end of the world.

Who? The voice of the poet – but the commentary that follows suggests the implied presence of other people.

When? The sonnets were published in 1609, but most scholars believe that Shakespeare began to write them in the 1590s. Within the poem no particular time is specified.

Where? No particular place is specified, so the location does not seem important.

What? Shakespeare states that true love will never change and then explores this assertion through a series of images in order to prove or demonstrate that love will never change.

Commentary

The opening sentence of the sonnet is justly famous: the recurrence of the letter *m* which both alliterates and is within certain words and the way the first line runs on into the second

Let me not to the marriage of true minds

Admit impediments

creates a gentle, calm, mellifluous tone which is appropriate to the sense: assonance on the letter *l* allows creates euphony, which is all enhanced by the enjambment. The next sentence too

Love is not love

Which alters when it alteration finds.

is often quoted on its own and offered as a universal truth: true love never changes no matter what happens. This second sentence is memorable not just because of the sentiment but because of the words: the repetition of the word *love* as well as *alter/alteration* and the soft sounds of the letter *l* and *w* and *f*. So far the sonnet is quite clearly concerned with marriage and *alters* is a pun on what we find at the eastern end of a church the altar. *Impediment* too is a word, a very important word, in the Church of England marriage service. In the marriage service the priest says to the congregation, before the couple exchange their vows of marriage:

Does anyone know of any just cause or impediment why these two should not be joined together in holy matrimony?

Impediment here means an obstacle. At this point in the service, centuries ago, this was the moment when someone in the congregation could mention an obstacle – such one of the couple being already married or promised to someone else or below the legal age to marry or whatever. The final line of the quatrain continues this pattern of repetition – *remover/remove*.

The second quatrain introduces new images in an effort to define what love is. Line 5 begins with a dramatic exclamation – *O no* – and then introduces a metaphor based on ships and navigation. Love is *ever-fixèd*: it never changes and can endure the fury of tempests without being shaken; love is like a star that guides sailors who would otherwise be lost (*wandering*) and they measure the height of the star (love) even before they understand whether the star will help them navigate. Shakespeare uses assonance – *star* assonates with the rhyme words *bark* and *mark* – and *whose worth's unknown* – repeats the same sound with *o* – which also goes back to the exclamation at the start of the quatrain. This creates a sort of aural harmony even though he is writing about potentially dangerous things – tempests, and ships that are lost.

The third quatrain changes the line of thought again. It starts with a bold statement – *Love's not Time's fool*; Shakespeare means that true love will not alter even though time changes our physical appearance as we age. Time destroys *rosy lips and cheeks*. Note the consonance on *c* in *sickle's compass come*. Line 11 deliberately echoes the opening quatrain with its use of *alters*. The whole quatrain is held together not just by sense and subject matter and rhyme, but also alliteration – *bending, brief, but bears*. The final line says that love will last until Doomsday, the end of time.

The sonnet ends with an assertive couplet. Shakespeare states that if he is wrong – that if love is impermanent or transitory then it follows that he, the poet, never wrote a word and no human being ever really loved.

This poem is usually read as a definition of love or true love: an emotion that survives time and tempests, that will never change, no matter what happens. This is why it is so popular in connection with marriages – it serves, people think, as a vow of love that will last forever. Perhaps its power has a lot to do with its sounds: we have noted the clever use of repetition; the euphony created by the soft consonants in the opening quatrain; and, perhaps, its appeal has something to do with Shakespeare's straightforward imagery of stars and ships, rosy cheeks, death personified with his bending sickle. However, a closer reading will show that there is another possibility, another way to interpret this very famous poem.

Remember that in the first sentence Shakespeare had said he was not going to admit impediments – he is going to say nothing at this point of the marriage service. This suggests that Shakespeare is writing about the marriage of someone else and asserting that he still loves that person and his love will never change, despite the fact that they are marrying someone else and not him. It is ironic, isn't it, that the sonnet is so often used in marriage services: this is a poem about the end of a relationship – a relationship that is ending because one of the people involved in the relationship is getting married. Consequently, the speaker's feelings are of sadness and a sense of betrayal, but they are controlled by the strict form of the sonnet which helps to restrain the terrible sadness the speaker feels.

In the light of this reading of the poem, the poem's imagery still fits with what I wrote earlier in the summary, but some of the images take on a darker, sadder tone and atmosphere. The simile involving the *wandering bark* works as a simile, but it might also suggest Shakespeare's emotional state now that his former lover has rejected him to marry someone else – he is like a ship drifting. Love that bears it out until the edge of doom, means a love that will never die and will keep going until Doomsday, but that word *doom* perhaps suggests the terrible sadness that Shakespeare feels at the end of the relationship: in a sense it is almost like the end of the world for him. *Bears it out* suggests a determination to keep going despite the heartbreak he feels – and he does, in a sense, keep going, because the sonnet reaches its conclusion.

Why?

This world-famous poem

- offers a definition of love which many readers have found comforting and inspiring.

- asserts that true love lasts forever and will endure absence and time and even death.

- uses simple repetition and wonderfully crafted combinations of sound to create euphony.

BUT it might also be read as

- a poem full of heartbreak and sadness at the loss of a loved one who marries someone else.

Here is the second poem that we will look at as an unseen:

The Sick Rose

O rose, thou art sick!
  The invisible worm,
That flies in the night,
  In the howling storm,

Has found out thy bed   5
  Of crimson joy,
And his dark secret love
  Does thy life destroy

thou – you

thy - your

Who? The voice of the poet, the invisible worm, a rose.

When? In the night during a storm.

Where? Hard to say... in the bed of the rose.

What? Just using what we know from the poem, we can say that an invisible worm discovers the dark secret love of the rose and destroys it during a storm.

It is obvious that this method will not get us very far with this type of poem or, at least, will not get us beyond a superficial interpretation of what it means. Before you read any further, please read my comments below about William Blake's poem 'London', on page 40 because Blake is also the author of 'The Sick Rose'.

What can we say with any certainty about this poem? Its mood is sinister. It is night-time and there is a howling storm. An invisible worm has found out where the rose has its bed and is coming to take its life. *Found out* suggests that the bed needs to be hidden. Paradoxically, although the worm is going to destroy the life of the rose, the worm has a *dark secret love* for the rose: this is now especially disturbing – a love which is dark and secret and which is destructive of life. Not only is it night and, therefore, dark, but the love of the worm is also dark and secret and destructive. We expect love to be a positive emotion which brings good things to our lives.

When faced with this poem many readers want to interpret the poem symbolically – otherwise it becomes a poem about horticulture. The poem is full of words that we associate with love - *rose, bed, joy, love*. In addition, in our culture sending someone roses, especially red roses, is a token of love. But this is a love which has gone wrong and is destructive. Many readers also find the shape of the worm rather phallic – suggestive of the penis. Think of all the types of love which might be considered 'wrong' or destructive. This is the list I came up with, but I am sure you can think of many others:

- Love for someone who does not love you back.

- Love for someone who is already married or in a relationship.

- Love which cannot be expressed.

- Love that transmits disease through unprotected sex.

- Love between two people from different religions.

- Love which is against the law.

- Love which is unwanted by the person you love.

- Love between two people of different class backgrounds.

- Love between two people of the same gender.

- Love or sexual expressions of love which are condemned by the church or by religious doctrine or law.

- Love which is possessive and selfish.

The point of this list is really to show that Blake's power of compression suggests a love that has gone wrong and leaves us to interpret it. To say that 'The Sick Rose' is about any one of the situations listed above would be totally wrong; to say that it suggests them all and encompasses them all, suggests the power of Blake's writing.

Furthermore, if you have read 'London' and its section later in this book and if you remember that the rose is the national symbol of England, then this poem becomes even more than a poem about love gone wrong – it becomes (perhaps) a poem about the state of England and a warning that it will soon be destroyed. You don't have to identify exactly what or who the worm is – the poem does that for you: the worm is destructive and capable of killing – it is a symbol of ALL the things Blake hated in his society. Blake's point is that the rose is sick and is about to be destroyed by sinister, invisible powers.

Finally, if you need any proof of Blake's power to compress meaning, just look at how many words I have used in an attempt to give meaning to his words: Blake uses (including the title) only thirty-seven! This is part of the poem's power and art – that it uses powerful words and imagery from which we can extract a multitude of meanings.

Why? This astonishingly compressed and darkly evocative poem is

- a protest about the England that Blake lived in.

- a protest about the way the church and society saw certain types of love as wrong.

- a warning that love – or what we call love- can be destructive if it is not fulfilled.

- a plea for tolerance and inclusion for those who conventional morality condemns.

The third poem we will examine is 'Porphyria's Lover' by Robert Browning, whose poem 'My Last Duchess' is in the anthology: when you have read them both you will be able to see interesting connections between the two poems.

'Porphyria's Lover' – Robert Browning

The rain set early in to-night,
    The sullen wind was soon awake,
It tore the elm-tops down for spite,
    And did its worst to vex the lake:
    I listened with heart fit to break.
When glided in Porphyria; straight
    She shut the cold out and the storm,
And kneeled and made the cheerless grate
    Blaze up, and all the cottage warm;
    Which done, she rose, and from her form
Withdrew the dripping cloak and shawl,
    And laid her soiled gloves by, untied

Her hat and let the damp hair fall,
    And, last, she sat down by my side
    And called me. When no voice replied,
She put my arm about her waist,
    And made her smooth white shoulder bare,
And all her yellow hair displaced,
    And, stooping, made my cheek lie there,
    And spread, o'er all, her yellow hair,
Murmuring how she loved me — she
    Too weak, for all her heart's endeavour,
To set its struggling passion free
    From pride, and vainer ties dissever,
    And give herself to me for ever.
But passion sometimes would prevail,
    Nor could to-night's gay feast restrain
A sudden thought of one so pale
    For love of her, and all in vain:
    So, she was come through wind and rain.
Be sure I looked up at her eyes
    Happy and proud; at last I knew
Porphyria worshipped me; surprise
    Made my heart swell, and still it grew
    While I debated what to do.
That moment she was mine, mine, fair,
    Perfectly pure and good: I found
A thing to do, and all her hair
    In one long yellow string I wound
    Three times her little throat around,
And strangled her. No pain felt she;

I am quite sure she felt no pain.
As a shut bud that holds a bee,
 I warily oped her lids: again
 Laughed the blue eyes without a stain.
And I untightened next the tress
 About her neck; her cheek once more
Blushed bright beneath my burning kiss:
 I propped her head up as before,
 Only, this time my shoulder bore
Her head, which droops upon it still:
 The smiling rosy little head,
So glad it has its utmost will,
 That all it scorned at once is fled,
 And I, its love, am gained instead!
Porphyria's love: she guessed not how
 Her darling one wish would be heard.
And thus we sit together now,
 And all night long we have not stirred,
 And yet God has not said a word!

Context

Robert Browning was born in 1812 and became one of the most famous English poets of the Victorian era. He was married to Elizabeth Barrett Browning who was a semi-invalid with an over-protective father. The couple were married in secret and then went to live in Italy. Browning's best work is often set in the past and he was a master of the dramatic monologue, in which the imagined speaker of the poem reveals their innermost thoughts and feelings, often going on to uncover uncomfortable truths about themselves.

porphyria – a rare disorder of the blood that may cause mental, nervous or skin problems.

vex – annoy, anger.

soiled – dirty, unclean.

dissever – to separate, to part in two.

oped – opened.

tress – a long lock of hair.

Who? The poem is a dramatic monologue spoken by the male lover of Porphyria.

When? One dark stormy might. Browning uses the weather as a pathetic fallacy for the turbulent human emotions in the cottage.

Where? In an isolated cottage.

What? The speaker, without a word of explanation or regret, tells of Porphyria's visit to him and his subsequent murder of her. The speaker spends the night alone with the body of his dead lover.

Commentary

'Porphyria's Lover' by Robert Browning dramatizes the conflicts between social pressures and romantic love; the tension between female submissiveness and the male urge to possess, to control and to act; the tension between momentary pleasure and the human need to preserve and keep that transitory pleasure; and the tension between strong religious faith and religious doubt.

In 'Porphyria's Lover' Browning presents a speaker who is insane. The poem was originally published in 1836 in the London journal *Monthly Repository* (Hawlin, 44) and was paired with another poem with an identical rhyme scheme, metre, line length and overall length (Ryals,

166). The paired poems were printed under the title 'Madhouse Cells' and the other poem, 'Johannes Agricola in Meditation', shares a similar preoccupation to 'Porphyria's Lover' – what Ryals calls the desire or will for 'total possession of another person' (166).

The poem is a dramatic monologue – a type of poem that Browning would continue to write throughout his career, but in this early example the monologue seems to be addressed to the reader; later dramatic monologues, such as 'My Last Duchess' and 'Fra Lippo Lippi' where Browning developed the form by including within the poem other characters to whom the monologue is addressed (Ryals, 87). In 'Porphyria's Lover' the speaker is isolated in many ways as we will see. The speaker is recounting the events of the previous evening, so the poem is written after the main event of the poem (which Browning, as the poet, cleverly delays until line 42.). The speaker – the lover of Porphyria – has a tender tone as he recounts the events of the previous evening: indeed, Hawlin comments that his 'whole perspective is... gentle or feminized' (46). However, the speaker is also mad, and the crucial event of the poem in line 42, throws his previous solicitude and apparent love and care for Porphyria into a dark and deadly ironic light.

Browning's monologues are frequently voiced by eccentrics, lunatics, or people under emotional stress. Their ramblings illustrate character by describing the interactions of an odd personality with a particularly telling set of circumstances. In both 'Porphyria's Lover' and 'My Last Duchess', Browning uses this mode of exposition to describe a man who responds to the love of a beautiful woman by killing her. Each monologue offers the speakers' reasons for the desired woman from subject to object: in 'My Last Duchess', the Duke may have jealously murdered his wife, but keeps a portrait of her behind a curtain so no-one can look upon her smile without his permission; in 'Porphyria's Lover', the persona wishes to stop time at a single perfect moment and so kills his lover and sits all night embracing her carefully arranged body. It should be noted that in 'My Last Duchess' the woman's murder is at best implied, while in 'Porphyria's Lover' it is described quite explicitly by the speaker. The unchanging rhythmic pattern may also suggest the persona's insanity.

The 'Porphyria' persona's romantic egotism leads him into all manner of monstrously selfish assumptions compatible with his own longings. He seems convinced that Porphyria wanted to be murdered, and claims 'No pain felt she' while being strangled, adding, as if to convince himself, 'I am quite sure she felt no pain.' He may even believe she enjoyed the pain, because he, her lover, inflicted it. When she's dead, he says she's found her 'utmost will,' and when he sees her lifeless head drooping on his shoulder, he describes it as a 'smiling rosy little head', possibly using the word 'rosy' to symbolise the red roses of love, or to demonstrate his delusion that the girl, and their relationship, are still alive. More likely, however, is the thought that blood returning to her face, after the strangulation, makes her cheeks 'rosy.' Her 'rosy little head' may also be a sly reference to the hymen; Porphyria leaves a 'gay feast' and comes in from the outside world wearing 'soiled gloves'; now her blue eyes, open in death, are 'without a stain.' The lover may also be a fetishist, indicated by the fact that he refers to her hair numerous times throughout the poem, and strangles her with it. He also refers to the 'shut bud that holds a bee' which backs up the view of it being a sexual fetish.

It is impossible to know the true nature of his relationship to Porphyria. An incestuous relationship has been suggested; Porphyria might be the speaker's mother or sister. Another possibility is that she is a former lover, now betrothed, or even married, to some other man. Alternatively, they may be divided by social class.

Other sources speculate that the lover might be impotent, disabled, sick, or otherwise inadequate, and, as such, unable to satisfy Porphyria. There is much textual evidence to support this interpretation: he describes himself as 'one so pale / for love of her, and all in vain.' At the beginning of the poem, the persona never moves; he sits passively in a cold, dark room, sadly listening to the storm until Porphyria comes through 'wind and rain', 'shuts the cold out and the storm,' and makes up his dying fire. Finally, she sits beside him, calls his name, places his arm around her waist, and puts his head on her shoulder; interestingly, she has to stoop to do this. She is active; he is passive – suggesting impotence perhaps. At the poem's midpoint, the persona suddenly takes action, strangling Porphyria, propping her body against his, and boasting that afterwards, *her* head lay on *his* shoulder.

In line with the persona's suggested weakness and sickness, other scholars take the word 'porphyria' literally, and suggest that the seductress embodies a disease, and that the persona's killing of her is a sign of his recovery. Porphyria, which usually involved delusional madness and death, was classified several years before the poem's publication; Browning, who had an avid interest in such pathologies, may well have been aware of the new disease, and used it in this way to express his knowledge.

Much has been made of the final line: 'And yet, God has not said a word!' Possibly, the speaker seeks divine approval for the murder. He may believe God has said nothing because He is satisfied with his actions. God may be satisfied because: He recognises that the persona's crime is the only way to keep Porphyria pure; or, because He doesn't think her life and death are important compared to the persona's. The persona may also be waiting in vain for some sign of God's approval. Alternatively, the line may represent his feelings of emptiness in the wake of his violence; Porphyria is gone, quiet descends, and he's alone. The persona may also be **schizophrenic**; he may be listening for a voice in his head, which he mistakes for the voice of God. It has also been postulated that this is Browning's statement of 'God's silence,' in which neither good nor bad acts are immediately recompensed by the deity.

The final line may also register the persona's sense of guilt over his crime. Despite his elaborate justifications for his act, he has, in fact, committed murder, and he expects God to punish him – or, at least, to take notice. The persona is surprised, perhaps a little uneasy, at God's continued silence. An alternative reading of the last line is to identify a slightly gleeful tone in it – confirming once again that the speaker is insane.

There is no doubt of his insanity; exactly why he kills Porphyria is open to debate and interpretation.

The poem is set in an isolated rural cottage: Browning implies this because Porphyria who has walked through a storm to meet her lover is completely wet and immediately takes off her 'dripping cloak and shawl' (line 11) and her 'soiled gloves' (line 12). Browning uses the storm as a pathetic fallacy in at least three ways: firstly, it is an effective contrast with the warmth and love within the cottage once Porphyria lights the fire and makes advances to her lover; secondly, it can be seen as Browning foreshadowing the later, violent events of the poem; and, thirdly, it might even be seen as symbolizing the tortured inner feelings of Porphyria's 'murderously jealous lover' (Hair & Kennedy, 88) – feelings which he keeps under careful control. Knoepflmacher argues that Browning presents very well the 'contrast between a cold outside world and a warm interior' (158) and Porphyria herself can be seen as 'the passionate outsider penetrating that interior who brings warmth to the immobile dreamer within' (158). However, this can be seen as an example of prolepsis, since, despite the speaker's self-delusional assertions, in death Porphyria's body will rapidly lose all its warmth.

The relationship between the two lovers is presented by Browning as a clandestine one, but one which Porphyria wants: she has, after all, braved a storm to visit her lover and the way she 'put my arm about her waist,/And made her smooth white shoulder bare' (lines 16 -17) clearly suggests that the relationship is sexual. It seems that Browning suggests that it has to be clandestine because Porphyria and her lover are from different classes: Martens asserts that the poem is essentially about a man's 'pathological love for a socially-superior woman' (39). Browning suggests this through the speaker's words: he says that Porphyria is 'too weak… from pride' (lines 22 & 24) – presumably a pride issuing from her social superiority and the disgrace she would suffer if her love for this man became known, and he goes on to say that she is 'too weak' (line 22) to allow her 'struggling passion free' (line 23) and 'give herself to me forever' (line 25), because she is socially bound by what the speaker dismisses as 'vainer ties' (line 24) – presumably her sense of responsibility to her family. Browning presents the speaker as being very distraught at this situation: it explains why he does not respond in line 15 when she calls him and he comments that, because he cannot have her forever or is dependent on her secret visits to him, it seems that his love for her is 'all in vain' (line 30). But passion prevails – Browning hints perhaps that they make love and, as they do so, the man notices how Porphyria is looking at him and realizes 'I knew/Porphyria worshipped me' (lines 33 -34). He goes on:' That moment she was mine, mine, fair,/Perfectly pure and good' (line 38). But it is only a moment of intense feeling and, given what Browning has suggested about the nature of their relationship and his dependence on her coming to him when she can and not when she or he both want, he decides to preserve the moment and strangles her with her own hair. The repeated 'mine, mine' in line 37 convey his extreme possessiveness and Knoepflmacher writes that 'by draining Porphyria of her life, he can assume… control' (160). This can easily be seen as symptomatic of the masculine desire to possess and control, the human desire to preserve forever a moment of happiness, and we might even see the speaker as rebelling against a rigid class system which keeps him and his lover apart. However, by killing Porphyria, Browning presents the insane speaker as having wholly abrogated all moral responsibility for his actions and acted in defiance of human law and morality.

Mirroring the speaker's desire for control, the poem's structure is highly controlled. On the page the poem looks highly regular and it is: Browning conveys his speaker's thoughts with a regular unvarying rhyme scheme which consists of units of five lines which rhyme ABABB, CDCDD and so on. This tightly-controlled and very regular rhyme scheme could be said to mirror the speaker's own need for control and his obsession with Porphyria; at the same time, despite the horrific nature of his crime, his speaking voice remains calm and untroubled – just as the poem is very formally and regularly structured. Hawlin (42) describes the rhyme scheme as 'assymetrical' – presumably meaning that we might expect the six line unit to rhyme like this – ABABAB – but the rhyme scheme that Browning has chosen with the fifth and sixth line rhyming with each other, means that in terms of rhyme, the six line unit turns back on itself – an attempt surely to accentuate the self-obsessed, inward-looking nature of the speaker. In other words, the speaker is concerned only with his own feelings, despite his apparent concern for Porphyria – (No pain felt she;/I am quite sure she felt no pain' (lines 42 – 43). As Bailey asserts, the speaker has a 'megalomaniac stance towards his lover' (53), and he is 'self-deceiving' (Hair & Kennedy, 88). This self-deception and the evidence of his insanity continues after Porphyria is dead: the speaker thinks that her eyes 'laughed… without a stain' (line 46) and that 'her cheek once more/Blushed bright beneath my burning kiss' (lines 48 -49).

Browning uses a lot of enjambment – twenty-two times in a poem of sixty lines - so that over a third of the lines run on and are not end-stopped. On the one hand, it could be said that this enjambment helps convey the impression of a real voice that is speaking, but there is perhaps another purpose: in so many lines the words and syntax break through the end of the line and this is a poem about a speaker who breaks accepted morality by committing murder. Furthermore, the lines which build up to and describe Porphyria's murder – lines 32 to 42 – use an excessive amount of enjambment which perhaps help to convey the speaker's frenzy, emphasize his breaking of the rules and quicken the rhythm of the poem to its climax, as well as imitating the speedy act of strangling his lover. Browning's use of heavy, full-stop caesuras is equally significant. He uses only two: one in line 15 after Prophyria 'sat down by my side/And called me.' (lines 14 – 15) – a caesura which is used to emphasize the speaker's lack of response to her; the second in line 42 after 'strangled her' – which again serves, for the reader, to emphasize the enormity of the crime he has committed. The caesura helps to foreground the act of murder. However, Browning presents the speaker as so delusional that he argues that in killing his lover he was doing what she would have wanted: he describes her head as 'so glad it has its utmost will' (line 54) and he claims in his insanity that his killing of her is 'her darling one wish' (line 58). The speaker's final observation – that on the subject of the murder 'God has not said a word!' (line 60) – certainly shows the speaker's contempt and insouciance towards religious diktats forbidding murder.

Browning's 'Porphyria's Lover' is a deeply disturbing poem, enhanced by the strict regularity of the rhyme scheme and the control that Browning exerts over it. What appears to be a passionate story of the secret tryst of two lovers turns into a tale of sudden and violent murder, and a crazed and deluded justification of it. Ryals states that 'there has been some disagreement as to whether the lover kills Porphyria because he loves her or hates her' (271): it could be argued that such a question is irrelevant because, love her or hate her, he seeks to possess her completely and forever. It can be seen that the poem raises other issues – the unfairness of the British class system, the habitual, historical male need to dominate and a growing scepticism about God – but these are overshadowed by the pathological and wholly solipsistic megalomania of the speaker.

Works Cited

Bailey, Suzanne. *Cognitive Style and Perceptual Difference in Browning's Poetry*. London: Routledge, 2010. Print.

Browning, Robert. 'Porphyria's Lover'. *Poetry Foundation*. Web. October 28th, 2013.

Hair, Donald S. & Kennedy, Richard S. *The Dramatic Imagination of Robert Browning: A Literary Life*. Columbia, Mi: University of Missouri Press, 2007. Print.

Hawlin, Stefan. *Robert Browning*. London: Routledge, 2012. Print.

Knoepflmacher, U. C. 'Projection of the Female Other: Romanticism, Browning and the Victorian Dramatic Monologue'. Pp. 147 – 168 in Claridge, Laura & Langland, Elizabeth (eds.). *Out of Bounds: Male Writers and Gendered Criticism*. Boston, Ma: University of Massachusetts Press, 1990. Print.

Martens, Britta. *Browning, Victorian Poetics and the Romantic Legacy: Challenging the Personal Voice*. London: Aldgate Publishing Ltd, 2011. Print.

Ryals, Clyde de L. *Robert Browning: The Poems and Plays of Robert Browning, 1833 – 1846*. Columbus, Oh: Ohio State University Press, 1983. Print.

In 'Porphyria's Lover' Browning:

- uses dramatic monologue to present a solipsistic, psychopathic maniac;

- to suggest an illicit love affair, perhaps caused by social differences;

- uses a rigid rhyme scheme and metre to suggest the speaker's confidence and rigidity of thinking, but also uses caesura brilliantly at key moments;

- presents an insane mind obsessed with full possession of his lover;

- in the poem presents possessive love as a life-denying force.

Finally, we will look at a very famous poem called 'The Voice' by Thomas Hardy:

'The Voice'

Woman much missed, how you call to me, call to me,
Saying that now you are not as you were

When you had changed from the one who was all to me,
But as at first, when our day was fair.

Can it be you that I hear? Let me view you, then,
Standing as when I drew near to the town
Where you would wait for me: yes, as I knew you then,
Even to the original air-blue gown!

Or is it only the breeze, in its listlessness
Travelling across the wet mead to me here,
You being ever dissolved to wan wistlessness,
Heard no more again far or near?

    Thus I; faltering forward,
    Leaves around me falling,
Wind oozing thin through the thorn from norward,
    And the woman calling.

Context

listlessness – the state of being listless, lacking energy.

mead – meadow or field.

wan – pale.

wistlessness – 'to wist' is an old English verb meaning to know. So 'wistlessness' is literally the state of being no longer known.

Who? The poet speaks as himself, addressing his dead wife.

When? After his wife's death. The poem comes from a sequence known as *Poems 1912-13.*

Where? An outdoor setting suggested by the final stanza, the wet mead and the wind and the falling leaves.

What? The poet is haunted by the voice of his dead wife and he reminiscences about how happy they were at the start of their relationship. The final stanza breaks the pattern of the previous three stanzas to suggest Hardy's forlorn sadness, his heart-felt confusion and his lack of direction.

Before we can get to grips with this poem we need to know something about Hardy's personal life. In 1870, while on an architectural mission to restore the parish church of St Juliot in Cornwall (he was a trained architect), Hardy met and fell in love with Emma Lavinia Gifford, whom he married in 1874. In 1885 Thomas and his wife moved into Max Gate, a house Hardy had designed himself and his brother had built. Although they later became estranged and the love between them faded, her subsequent death in 1912 had a traumatic effect on him and after her death, Hardy made a trip to Cornwall to revisit places linked with their courtship; his *Poems 1912–13* reflect upon her death. In 1914, Hardy married his secretary Florence Emily Dugdale, who was 39 years his junior. However, he remained preoccupied with his first wife's death and tried to overcome his remorse by writing poetry. 'The Voice' is one of the most celebrated poems about his dead wife.

In the first stanza Hardy imagines the voice of his dead wife calling him. The first line is metrically very complex. It starts arrestingly with a trochaic foot – 'woman' – which is followed by an alliterative spondee – 'much missed' before ending the line on a falling dactylic metre – 'call to me, call to me' and the repetition of the words suggests that he keeps hearing her voice in his mind. The falling dactylic metre conjures up a mood of forlorn sadness and plangent regret, and Hardy uses the same way to end the first and third lines of the first three stanzas. The rest of the first stanza uses very simple English words to describe a complex emotional situation. Hardy imagines that his dead wife, Emma, is telling him that she has changed back to the person he knew when he first met her – 'as at first, when our day was fair'. In other words, she has changed from when their marriage developed problems – when she has changed from the one who was all to him – and has changed back to her original self.

The second stanza opens with a direct question: 'Can it be you that I hear?' – which is given added force by the caesura which follows it. If he can hear her voice, he wants to see her too – 'Let me view you then.' Hardy summons up an image of Emma when they had just met and she would wait for him on the edge of town. The last three syllables of the stanza are stressed – 'air-blue gown' – which suggests the striking immediacy of Hardy's memory and its force and clarity even though he is thinking of events from decades before.

There is a radical change of tone in the third stanza and the use of pathetic fallacy to present the way Hardy is feeling. He wonders whether it is not Emma's voice that he can hear at all but

...is it only the breeze, in its listlessness
Travelling across the wet mead to me here.

The dactyl which ends line one maintains the tone of febrile frailty and sadness: after all, Hardy knows that Emma is dead 'dissolved to wan wistlessness' and death is final: Emma is 'Heard no more again far or near' and the alliteration on 'w' and the sibilance of 'wan wistlessness' contributes to a subdued sense of sadness.

The final stanza breaks completely the pattern Hardy established in the first three: so great is his regret that he loses control of the shape and pattern of the poem. The first line is interesting:

Thus I; faltering forward

The caesura after 'Thus I' enacts Hardy's own faltering, while the alliteration on the soft 'f' suggests hesitation and frailty and is continued in the 'falling' of the leaves in the next line. There is pathetic fallacy too: it is autumn and the leaves are falling as a precursor to winter. The north wind is blowing too so it will be very cold. The line:

Wind oozing thin through the thorn from norward

is an interesting combination of vowel sounds with short 'i' sounds (wind and thin) contrasting with longer 'o' (*oozing, through, thorn, norward*) which suggests the wind gusting through the thick thorn bush. There is also alliteration on 'th' – a difficult sound to say and which stresses the effort with which the wind blows. The poem ends where it began with 'the woman calling'.

There is something grammatically interesting about the last stanza too: technically it is not a complete sentence because it contains no finite verb – there is no completed action which suggests that there is no escape for Hardy from these feelings and that he will always hear Emma's voice, always regret how their marriage fell apart. All the verbs Hardy uses are non-finite, present participles – 'faltering', 'falling', 'oozing', 'calling' – which suggest a never-ending sequence of events that he cannot control (after all he is 'faltering'). Hardy also ends each line of the last stanza with a trochaic foot and this falling, feminine rhythm also contributes to its sadness.

This poem shows Hardy at the height of his powers as a poet.

Endings

This may seem like an obvious point, one hardly worth drawing attention to, but you have seen from the poems discussed above that the endings of poems are absolutely vital and crucial to their overall effect. In 'The Sick Rose' the final word – *destroy* – carries threat and menace. You will find in many of the poems in the Anthology the ending – the final stanza, the final line, the final sentence, even sometimes the final word – changes what has gone before and forces us to see things differently. So be aware of this as you read and as you revise. When you are writing about poems, the way they end and the emotional conclusion they achieve is a simple way to compare and contrast them. It may not be easy to express what it is exactly that they do achieve, but make sure you write something about the endings, because the endings are often the key to the whole poem. Remember – a poem (like a song) is an emotional journey and the destination, the ending, is part of the overall message, probably its most important part.

'La Belle Dame sans Merci: A Ballad' – John Keats

Author & Context

John Keats (31 October 1795 – 23 February 1821) was an English Romantic poet. He was one of the main figures of the second generation of Romantic poets along with Lord Byron and Percy Bysshe Shelley, despite his work having been in publication for only four years before his death. Although his poems were not generally well-received by critics during his life, his reputation grew after his death, so that by the end of the 19th century, he had become one of the most beloved of all English poets. He had a significant influence on a diverse range of poets and writers.

The poetry of Keats is characterised by sensual imagery, most notably in the series of odes. Today his poems and letters are some of the most popular and most analysed in English literature. Keats suffered from tuberculosis, for which, at the time, there was no cure and as a result, perhaps, many of his poems are tinged with sadness and thoughts of mortality, as well as having a keen eye for the beauties of nature and the pains of unrequited love.

La Belle Dame sans Merci – the beautiful woman without pity.

what can ail thee – what can trouble or afflict you.

loitering -waiting around with no fixed purpose.

sedge – a type of grass whish flourishes in watery places.

woe-begone – consumed with woe and sadness.

meads – meadows and fields.

steed – his horse.

manna – delicious food for body and mind.

grot – a cave.

in thrall – to be held like a slave.

gloam – twilight, dusk.

sojourn – to stay for a period of time.

Who? An unidentified speaker asks a knight-at-arms what is wrong with him: he or she speaks for the first three stanzas. The knight then tells his story.

When? The knight and the people he sees in his dream suggest a medieval setting, centuries before Keats was alive.

Where? An indeterminate outdoor setting: the knight says he is on the cold hill's side and the setting is rural.

What? The knight met La Belle Dame Sans Merci of the title. They seemed to fall in love and she took him to her grot. He fell asleep and dreamt a dream before walking up on the cold hillside, alone and deeply sad.

Commentary

This is one of hundreds of anonymous ballads which were passed down orally before being written down.

Lady Maisrey

She called to her little pageboy,
Who was her brother's son.
She told him quick as he could go,
To bring her lord safe home.

Now the very first mile he would walk
And the second he would run,

And when he came to a broken, broken bridge,
He bent his breast and swum.

And when he came to the new castell,
The lord was set at meat;
If you were to know as much as I,
How little you would eat!

O is my tower falling, falling down,
Or does my bower burn?
Or is my gay lady put to bed
With a daughter or a son?

O no, your tower is not falling down,
Nor does your bower burn;
But we are afraid ere you return,
Your lady will be dead and gone.

Come saddle, saddle my milk-white steed,
Come saddle my pony too,
That I may neither eat nor drink,
Till I come to the old castell.

Now when he came to the old castell,
He heard a big bell toll;
And then he saw eight noble, noble men,
A bearing of a pall.

Lay down, lay down, that gentle, gentle corpse,
As it lay fast asleep,
That I may kiss her red ruby lips,
Which I used to kiss so sweet.

Six times he kissed her red ruby lips,

Nine times he kissed her chin.
Ten times he kissed her snowy, snowy breast,
Where love did enter in.

The lady was buried on that Sunday,
Before the prayer was done;
And the lord he died on the next Sunday,
Before the prayer begun.

I have included this anonymous ballad to give you a sense of the tradition Keats was drawing on when he wrote 'La Belle Dame Sans Merci'. It is also written in the traditional ballad stanza. I chose it also because it involves love and death, and a way of telling the story which is elliptical – in which important parts are left out and the readers are left to their own conclusions. Keats' poem is filled with such features.

"La Belle Dame sans Merci" is a popular form given an artistic sheen by the Romantic poet, Keats. Keats uses a stanza of three iambic tetrameter lines with the fourth line shortened which makes the stanza seem a self-contained unit, giving the ballad a deliberate and slow movement, and is pleasing to the ear although the short last line could also be argued to add an air of doubt, of uncertainty and incompleteness. Keats uses a number of the stylistic characteristics of the ballad, such as simplicity of language, repetition, and absence of details; like some of the old ballads, it deals with the supernatural. Keats's economical manner of telling a story in "La Belle Dame sans Merci" is the direct opposite of his lavish manner in "The Eve of St. Agnes". Part of the fascination exerted by the poem comes from Keats' use of understatement. It is a love story, but not a happy or uncomplicated one. The shortened last line suggests a lack of completeness and, as such, is appropriate to the events of the poem and the overall sense of melancholy and anguish that pervades it. The poem became famous in the Victorian period and several Pre-Raphaelite artists produced work inspired by the poem and reproduced here.

Keats sets his simple story of love and death in a bleak wintry landscape that is appropriate to it: *The sedge has wither'd from the lake/And no birds sing!* The repetition of these two lines, with minor variations, as the concluding lines of the poem emphasizes the fate of the unfortunate knight and neatly encloses the poem in a frame by bringing it back to its beginning. Keats relates the condition of the trees and surroundings with the condition of the knight who is also broken.

In keeping with the ballad tradition, Keats does not identify his questioner, or the knight, or the destructively beautiful lady. What Keats does not include in his poem contributes as much to it in arousing the reader's imagination as what he puts into it. La belle dame sans merci, the beautiful lady without pity, is a femme fatale, a Circe-like figure who attracts lovers only to destroy them by her supernatural powers. She destroys because it is her nature to destroy. Keats could have found patterns for his "faery's child" in folk mythology, classical literature, Renaissance poetry, or the medieval ballad. With a few skilful touches, he creates a woman who is at once beautiful, erotically attractive, fascinating, and deadly.

Some readers see the poem as Keats' personal rebellion against the pains of love. In his letters and in some of his poems, he reveals that he did experience the pains, as well as the pleasures, of love and that he resented the pains, particularly the loss of freedom that came with falling in love. However, the ballad is a very objective form, and it may be best to read "La Belle Dame sans Merci" as pure story and no more. Certainly the poem stands out from the others in the Anthology by having a clear narrative element – although the sadness that love can cause is touched upon in several different poems.

The first three stanzas of the poem are spoken by an unidentified speaker who questions the knight-at-arms. It is winter and the knight is clearly unwell:

I

O what can ail thee, knight-at-arms,
  Alone and palely loitering?
The sedge has wither'd from the lake,
  And no birds sing.

II

O what can ail thee, knight-at-arms!
  So haggard and so woe-begone?
The squirrel's granary is full,
  And the harvest's done.

III

I see a lily on thy brow
  With anguish moist and fever dew,
And on thy cheeks a fading rose
  Fast withereth too.

The lily is a flower associated with death, while on the knight's cheeks there is a *fading rose,* suggesting a fading or lost love. The questions serve the simple task of arousing the reader's interest, while the state of the knight is pitiful: he is *alone and palely loitering, haggard* and *woe-begone* and *anguish* is apparent on his fevered brow.

The knight then tells his story and how he has come to be in this situation. The knight met a lady *in the meads*; she was *full beautiful, a faery's child* (which introduces a supernatural element). It is clear that the knight is attracted to the woman and captivated by her appearance:

Her hair was long, her foot was light,

And her eyes were wild.

The knight shows his love for the woman by making a *garland* for her head and *bracelets* and

She looked at me as she did love,

And made sweet moan.

The word *as* is important in the quotation used above because it means she looked at him as if she did love him, but it does not mean that she necessarily does.. In the next stanza the knight seems to take full possession of the woman by placing her on his *prancing steed* and his obsession and infatuation with the woman is total:

And nothing else saw all day long,

For sidelong would she bend, and sing

A faery's song.

The faery's child, the woman, feeds the knight on *roots of relish sweet, / And honey wild. And manna-dew*

and then

...in language strange she said –

'I love thee true'.

The next stanza represents the climax of their love:

She took me to her Elfin grot,

And there she wept and sighed full sore.

And there I shut her wild wild eyes

With kisses four.

The kisses four feel like a consummation of their love and they certainly calm the wildness in her eyes. The woman lulls him to sleep and then the knight has a disturbing dream: *Ah! Woe betide!*:

I saw pale kings and princes too'

Pale warriors, death-pale were they all

They cried — 'La belle dame sans merci

Hath thee in thrall!'

I saw their starved lips in the gloam,

With horrid warning gapèd wide,

And I awoke to find me here

On the hill's cold side.

Of course, the wintry, lifeless landscape, underlined by the repetition of the *hill's cold side* acts as a pathetic fallacy for the knight's sense of futility and despondency.

The final stanza reminds us of the barrenness of the landscape:

And this is why I sojourn here,
Alone and palely loitering,
Though the sedge is withered from the lake,
And no birds sing.

A key word in the final stanza is *this* in the first line. Is the knight hoping to meet La belle dame sans merci again, once more to come under her spell? Is he so broken by his experiences that he can do nothing but palely loiter, enervated by the glimpse of love that he has seen but from which he is banished? Has his taste of love with the faery's child soured his feelings about love forever? Or has his taste of love left him bereft and lifeless until he tastes it again?

In his other poems Keats writes extensively about love. However, in 'La Belle Dame Merci', by choosing the impersonal ballad form, Keats distances himself personally from the poem and its sentiments. Nonetheless, a clear picture of love emerges through the unusual story of the knight and his encounter with La belle dame sans merci.

This poem is typical of some poems in the Anthology because it deals with the anguish and torment of unrequited love, but it is not typical in many more ways. It is set in a vague medieval past and the ballad form de-personalizes it and distances it from the poet's own feelings – most of the poems in the Anthology are deeply personal.

Why?

In this poem:

- Keats presents the anguish and torment of lost love.

- at the same time in stanzas VI, VII and VIII Keats presents the alluring pleasures of romantic love.

- uses the ballad form to present an intriguing story of a haggard knight at arms who has been broken in some way by love.

- successfully imitates the traditional ballad through his use of the ballad stanza, repetition, hints of the supernatural, illogical turns of events and the anonymity of the speakers.

- uses pathetic fallacy to great effect.

'A Child to his Sick Grandfather' - Joanna Baillie

Author

Joanna Baillie (11 September 1762 – 23 February 1851) was a Scottish poet and dramatist. Baillie was very well-known during her lifetime and, though a woman, intended her plays not for the closet but for the stage. Admired both for her literary powers and her sweetness of disposition, she hosted a literary society in her cottage at Hampstead. Baillie died at the age of 88, her faculties remaining unimpaired to the last. Baillie's lyric poems often take the form of meditations on nature and youth. She was the author of *Poems: Wherein It Is Attempted to Describe Certain Views of Nature and of Rustic Manners* (1790), *Metrical Legends of Exalted Characters* (1821), *Dramatic Poetry* (1836), and *Fugitive Verses* (1840).

Joanna Baillie was regarded as a pre-eminent woman poet in her lifetime, comparable to Sappho, and a forerunner of nineteenth-century British women's poetry. Elizabeth Barrett Browning hailed her as "the first female poet in all senses in England". But this poet was Scottish, wrote in Scots as well as English, and was a major contributor to the Scottish ballad and song revival. As Scullion remarks, "although so long resident in London, she was celebrated as a Scottish woman of letters" (161).

stocked – stocking or socks.

corse – body.

vexed – upset.

dad – here used as an abbreviation of 'grandad'.

wot – know.

lank -

scant – sparse, few in number.

crown – top of the head.

wan – pale.

doff – take off.

aye – always.

bide – wait.

partlet – a hen.

bosom – chest.

Who? The speaker is the grandson; his words are addressed to his grandfather. The poem is written in the present tense.

When? As his grandfather approaches death.

Where? In the family home it would seem.

What? The grandson's monologue is full of love and tenderness for his grandfather and he talks about things they have done together.

Commentary

This poem is written in eight stanzas of six lines each. Each verse is written in rhyming couplets, with the first seven lines in iambic tetrameters (four stresses with a generally iambic rhythm; the last line is slightly shorter – an iambic trimeter (three stresses). This rigid structure and the simple rhyme scheme are appropriate for a speaker who is a child and who sees things in simple terms.

In the first stanza the speaker notices that his grandad is *old and frail* and that his legs have begun *to fail*; indeed, he no longer uses his walking stick because it

Can scarce support your bended corse.

The speaker remembers a time when his grandfather's stick was used by the speaker as a pretend horse but now

While back to wall, you lean so sad,

I'm vexed to see you, dad.

In the second stanza the speaker reminisces

You used to smile and stroke my head,

And tell me how good children did.

But now his grandfather *seldom [takes him] on his knee*, but the speaker is

... right glad.

To sit beside you dad.

The speaker concentrates on his grandfather's physical decline in the third stanza:

How lank and thin your beard hangs down!

Scant are the white hairs on your crown;

How wan and hollow are your cheeks!

The speaker is watching the slow descent towards death of his beloved grandfather, but his love and compassion are made completely clear and are inherently touching:

... yet, for all his strength be fled,

I love my own old dad.

In stanza four the perspective shifts to the community they are living in: housewives are brewing potions (presumably to make the grandfather better or to reduce his suffering), while gossips come to ask for you, the child tells his grandfather. Furthermore

... good men kneel, and say their prayers;

And everybody looks so sad,

> *When you are ailing, dad.*

Despite the age of the speaker his attitude is not innocent: he knows what may be coming and the first line of the fifth stanza asks

You will not die and leave us then?

The speaker promises that the rest of the household will be quiet as the grandfather sleeps

And when you wake we'll aye be near

> *To fill old dad his cheer.*

The speaker makes various promises in the sixth stanza to lead his grandfather by the hand, to help him during meals and to sit and talk with him. Once again we get the impression of the tenderness of the child's compassion.

The seventh stanza goes into detail about a story that the speaker, the grandson will tell his grandfather about a chicken and a fox – because you love a story, dad?

The final stanza begins with a promise of

> *... a wondrous tale*

Of men all clad in coats of mail

With glittering swords....

But the end of life is near

... you nod, I think?

Your fixed eyes begin to wink;

Down on your bosom sinks your head —

You do not hear me, dad.

And so the grandfather dies, tragically and poignantly, being talked to by his grandson.

This is a good poem, simple and yet very effective, which shows a close bond between the different generations of a family, and the care that the child has for his dying grandfather. Baillie does not need to write any stanzas recounting the child's grief — we know from the poem and the closeness that they have shared in the past that the child will be bereft and disconsolate. Moreover, what can the child say except express his grief and sadness: this does not need to be written; Baillie is crediting her readers with basic empathy.

Why?

In this poem Baillie

- chooses a child's perspective which is typical of Romantic poetry as they valued the innocence of children very highly.
- imitates the child's voice and concerns accurately.
- writes a sad and moving poem, made more sad by the use of a child narrator.

'She Walks in Beauty' – Lord Byron

Author and Context

Lord George Gordon Byron (1788-1824) was as famous in his lifetime for his personality cult as for his poetry. He created the concept of the 'Byronic hero' - a defiant, melancholy young man, brooding on some mysterious, unforgivable event in his past. Byron's influence on European poetry, music, novel, opera, and painting has been immense, although the poet was widely condemned on moral grounds by some of his contemporaries.

George Gordon, Lord Byron, was the son of Captain John Byron, and Catherine Gordon. He was born with a club-foot and became extremely sensitive about his lameness. Byron spent his early childhood years in poor surroundings in Aberdeen, where he was educated until he was ten. After he inherited the title and property of his great-uncle in 1798, he went on to Dulwich, Harrow, and Cambridge, where he piled up debts and aroused alarm with bisexual love affairs. Staying at Newstead in 1802, he probably first met his half-sister, Augusta Leigh with whom he was later suspected of having an incestuous relationship.

In 1807 Byron's first collection of poetry, *Hours of Idleness* appeared. It received bad reviews. The poet answered his critics with the satire *English Bards and Scotch Reviewers* in 1808. Next year he took his seat in the House of Lords, and set out on his grand tour, visiting Spain, Malta, Albania, Greece, and the Aegean. Real poetic success came in 1812 when Byron published the first two cantos of *Childe Harold's Pilgrimage* (1812-1818). He became an adored character of London society; he spoke in the House of Lords effectively on liberal themes, and had a hectic love-affair with Lady Caroline Lamb. Byron's *The Corsair* (1814), sold 10,000 copies on the first day of publication. He married Anne Isabella Milbanke in 1815, and their daughter Ada was born in the same year. The marriage was unhappy, and they obtained legal separation next year.

When the rumours started to rise of his incest and debts were accumulating, Byron left England in 1816, never to return. He settled in Geneva with Percy Bysshe Shelley, Mary Wollstonecraft Shelley, and Claire Clairmont, who became his mistress. There he wrote the two cantos of *Childe Harold* and "The Prisoner of Chillon". At the end of the summer Byron continued his travels, spending two years in Italy. During his years in Italy, Byron wrote *Lament of Tasso*, inspired by his visit to Tasso's cell in Rome, *Mazeppa* and started *Don Juan*, his satiric masterpiece.

After a long creative period, Byron had come to feel that action was more important than poetry. He armed a brig, the Hercules, and sailed to Greece to aid the Greek rebels, who had risen against their Ottoman overlords. However, before he saw any serious military action, Byron contracted a fever from which he died in Missolonghi on 19 April 1824. Memorial services were held all over the land. Byron's body was returned to England but was refused burial by the deans of both Westminster and St Paul's. Finally, Byron's coffin was placed in the family vault at Hucknall Torkard, near Newstead Abbey in Nottinghamshire.

climes — a country or region.

raven — a bird with jet black plumage.

tress – a plait or braid of hair.

o'er - over.

Who? Byron writes as himself. The poem is about Mrs John Wilmot, who was in mourning and was Byron's cousin by marriage.

When? Sometime in 1813 – it is said that Byron wrote the poem the morning after meeting Mrs Wilmot and it was published in *Hebrew Melodies* in 1814.

Where? At night at an evening function.

What? The poet praises the lady's beauty and links it to the purity of her character.

Commentary

"She Walks in Beauty" is a poem written in 1813 by Lord Byron, and is one of his most famous works. It was one of several poems to be set to Jewish tunes from the synagogue by Isaac Nathan, which were published as *Hebrew Melodies* in 1815.

It is said to have been inspired by an event in Byron's life: while at a ball, Byron met Anne Hathaway (Mrs Wilmot), his cousin by marriage through John Wilmot. She was in mourning, wearing a black dress set with spangles, as in the opening lines;

> *She walks in beauty, like the night*
> *Of cloudless climes and starry skies*

He was struck by her unusual beauty, and the next morning the poem was written.

'She Walks in Beauty' is not typical of the love poems of the past, because it is largely descriptive. Indeed, it is a poem in which we get a sense of what the woman looks like and what she is wearing. Furthermore, in many love poems of the past (and some in the Anthology) are very intimate: the poet addresses the female recipient of the poem. But not in this poem: the speaker's audience is anyone who reads the poem. Byron's poem attempts to praise the appearance and moral purity of the woman he is writing about. In many other love poems, we learn little about the woman involved, but that is not true of Byron's poem. In many of the love poems of the past there is an emphasis on the poet's feelings: in Byron's poem his feelings are implied perhaps, but completely subservient to his description of the woman the poem is about. Unusually for a love poem, we get a real sense of what the woman is like. Byron's feelings towards her are not like many love poems of the past where the male writers are obsessed with their feelings or seducing the woman into bed. The poem comes across as objective praise by a disinterested observer. Furthermore, it also subverts the convention that beautiful women have fair hair and are blonde in complexion – although many of Shakespeare's sonnets are addressed to the so-called Dark Lady of the sonnets.

The poem is written in iambic tetrameters with only one variation: the opening trochaic foot of line 4.

Byron begins the poem with a simple simile: Mrs Wilmot is like the night and the alliteration in the second line foregrounds the image still further. Byron then indulges in hyperbole by claiming that

All that's best of dark and bright

Meet in her aspect and her eyes.

She is lit by moonlight and starlight which Byron which Byron calls a *tender light* which is denied to *gaudy day*, gaudy being used pejoratively.

The second stanza stresses the absolute perfection of her appearance:

One shade the more, one ray the less

would have *impaired* the beauty of this woman. Byron claims she has a *nameless grace / Which waves in every raven tress* and he links her external beauty with her inner thoughts and feelings, claiming that in her face one can discern

... thoughts serenely sweet [which] express

How pure, how dear their dwelling place.

The third stanza is full of praise for the recipient of the poem. Byron says that on her *cheeks* and on her *brow* - which are *so soft, so calm, yet eloquent,* are

The smiles that win, the tints that glow,

But tell of days in goodness spent.

In short, according to Byron's poem, she is the perfect woman: perfect in looks and in personality, character and intellect. She has

A mind at peace with all below,

A heart whose love is innocent.

Why is this such a famous poem?

- Byron acts as an objective observer so we are more likely to believe him.
- the regular iambic tetrameters do not distract from the harmony of the woman he describes – in fact, they enhance it and make it easy to memorize.
- the night-time setting is romantic and links with Mrs Wilmot's hair and complexion.
- the language is simple and easy to understand.
- Byron uses alliteration throughout but in an unobtrusive way.
- Byron establishes a clear link between the woman's beauty and her character – something unique in this Anthology.

Further reading: *Hebrew Melodies* ISBN: 978-1511897449

'A Complaint' – William Wordsworth
Author and Context

William Wordsworth was born in 1770 in Cockermouth on the edge of the English Lake District. He had a life-long fascination with nature and it is from the natural world that he took much of his inspiration. He died in 1850, having been made Poet Laureate in 1843. Wordsworth began to write *The Prelude* in 1798 and kept working on it and revising it until his death. It was not published until 1850, three months after his death. He published many poems during his own lifetime, but many readers feel that *The Prelude* is his finest work.

In his early years as a poet he was very friendly with the English poet Samuel Taylor Coleridge. In 1798 they published together a collection of poems called *Lyrical Ballads* with a longer version being published in 1800. Lyrical Ballads was to prove one of the most influential collections of poetry and Wordsworth and Coleridge collaborated closely over it. However, the years passed and disagreements between the two poets became bitter and they were estranged. This poem is Wordsworth's reaction to that failed friendship.

Who? Wordsworth writes about the breakdown of his friendship with Samuel Taylor Coleridge – at least it is widely assumed that the poem is about Wordsworth's relationship with Coleridge. The two poets had been very close during the 1790s and had collaborated together.

fond – affectionate.

When? In the early years of the nineteenth century.

Where? No specific location.

What? Wordsworth writes of the enormous inspiration that Coleridge gave him and his sadness that their friendship has waned.

Commentary

This poem consists of three stanzas which have the same pattern: the first four lines form a quatrain, rhyming ABAB and the stanza ends with a rhyming couplet.

The first line sums up the current situation:

There is a change – and I am poor.

Wordsworth means poor in an intellectual or artistic sense. He goes on to praise Coleridge's influence on him by using the metaphor of a fountain, *Whose only business was to flow* and help and inspire Wordsworth in his writing. Coleridge's inspiration was vital to Wordsworth. He says of the fountain:

And flow it did; not taking heed

Of its own bounty, or my need.

The caesura in the fifth line helps to suggest that the *fountain* has stopped flowing, but Wordsworth clearly appreciated Coleridge's friendship, calling it a *bounty*.

The second stanza starts positively and pays tribute to Coleridge's influence as Wordsworth recalls the two poets' friendship and collaboration. The second stanza starts with two happy exclamations:

What happy moments did I count!

Blest was I then all bliss above!

However, the third line of the stanza starts with the word *Now* and Wordsworth proceeds to describe their current relationship. He begins by paying tribute to Coleridge, still using the metaphor of the fountain. He describes Coleridge's friendship as a

... consecrated fount

Of murmuring, sparkling, living love –

the three adjectives in this line showing the old intensity of their friendship and showing platonic love for Coleridge. But all this has changed:

What have I? shall I dare to tell?

A comfortless and hidden well.

The fountain bursting with energy has been replaced by a well – which brings no comfort and is hidden. Wells contain stagnant water; fountains gush and burst water everywhere – the metaphor is well-chosen.

In the final stanza Wordsworth holds out the hope that his relationship is not over by starting the final stanza:

A well of love – it may be deep –

I trust it is – and never dry.

Perhaps this is Wordsworth seeking some reconciliation with Coleridge. In the next two lines he appears to resign himself to the more distant relationship they now have:

What matter? If the waters sleep

In silence and obscurity.

However, in the final two lines he reveals his real feelings:

Such change, and at the very door

Of my fond heart, hath made me poor.

In terms of tone this poem is very varied: Wordsworth writes with real passion and enthusiasm about the past and Coleridge's deep impact on him; however, overall the tone is disconsolate and full of sadness at an intimacy that once meant so much has been allowed to decline from a fountain to a well. Perhaps Wordsworth intended the poem as a conciliatory gesture to revive their friendship.

Why?

In this poem of abandoned friendship Wordsworth:

- gives a vivid and passionate account of their former intimacy and friendship.
- uses natural imagery vividly to convey emotion.
- admits to uncertainty about how the friendship has declined.
- writes sadly about the loss of the friendship.

'Neutral Tones' – Thomas Hardy

Author and Context

 Thomas Hardy (1840 – 1928) is best known as a novelist. He wrote 15 novels, most of which are set largely in Dorset and the surrounding counties, and which deal with the ordinary lives of ordinary people in stories in which they struggle to find happiness and love – often battling against fate or their own circumstances. His final two novels *Tess of the D'Urbervilles* (1891) and *Jude the Obscure* (1895) both portray sex outside marriage in a sympathetic way and there was such a hysterical public outcry about the novels that Hardy stopped writing fiction and devoted the rest of his life to poetry. Although much of his poetry reflects his interest in nature and ordinary things, this poem is also typical of his work in that it is intensely personal and may reflect the intense unhappiness he felt in his first marriage.

Neutral – this can refer to the landscape, drained of vivid colours, but can also refer to the lovers in the poem – who are presented as being completely indifferent to one another.

Tones – like 'neutral' above this can refer to colour (or the lack of it), but also to the mood of the former lovers.

chidden – this is the past of 'to chide'. To chide means to tell off or to reprimand. Here it is as though God had told off the white sun.

sod – turf, the earth with grass on it.

rove – wander.

bird-a-wing – a bird in flight.

curst - cursed

Who? There is no reason to assume that the speaker is not Hardy himself. His lover is with him in the poem and this is seen in Hardy's use of the third person plural – 'we'.

When? On a cold winter's day. Hardy wrote the poem in 1867 at the age of 27, but it was not published until 1898.

Where? In the countryside beside a pond.

What? Hardy is looking back with bitterness and intense sadness at the end of a relationship.

Commentary

This is a bitter and pessimistic poem about the break-up of a relationship – one which Hardy remembers vividly and which still causes him pain and anguish. As a 'break up' poem, it is hard to think of a better one in the English Language – unless it's Byron's 'When We Two Parted'. Hardy uses pathetic fallacy throughout the poem, so the details of the weather and the landscape match and mirror the emotions of the two lovers.

The first stanza sets the scene. It is a bleak winter's day and the speaker and his former lover are standing by a pond. The landscape seems stripped of all fertility and strength. There are a few grey ash leaves scattered about and the sun, source of heat and light and life, is 'white, as though chidden of God' – chidden for being 'white' and for not offering any heat or real light on this miserable day? The sod is starving just as this relationship is starved now of any real love or affection.

In the second stanza Hardy directly addresses his lover, the first line using parallelism – 'eyes on me/eyes that rove'. Her eyes are like eyes that wander over 'tedious riddles of years ago' – suggesting that the relationship has been going on for years but that it has become 'tedious' – monotonous and uninteresting – a long time ago. They exchange some words (which Hardy does not bother to use in the poem) and he writes that the words they exchange – 'lost the more by our love': the words they speak now are trivial and meaningless and are in contrast to the love they once felt for each other. They are dull and irrelevant now (lost the more) in comparison with the love they once enjoyed (our love).

Hardy begins the third stanza with a scathing and oxymoronic simile by writing:

The smile on your mouth was the deadest thing

Alive enough to have strength to die –

which stresses the winter sterility of nature around them, but also accuses his lover of hypocrisy – why should she be smiling given the state of their relationship? Is it for form's sake or to try and keep up the pretence that they still mean something to each other? But then his lover makes 'a grin of bitterness' which is compared to 'an ominous bird-a-wing'. Some readers of Hardy have made the point that in his poems he uses birds in an ominous and usually pessimistic way – which is only interesting because it contrasts so sharply with the Romantic poets' use of birds in their poems. The Romantics (who preceded Hardy) almost always use birds as symbols of hope, poetic inspiration or the uplifting power of nature. Hardy – it could be argued – is more modern in his sensibility using birds as symbols of something negative and life-denying.

Hardy in the final stanza is writing from an imagined present and writes:

Since then, keen lessons that love deceives,

And wrings with wrong, have shaped to me

Your face, and the God-curst sun, and a tree

And a pond edged with grayish leaves.

'Since then' suggests the incident is long ago. Hardy suggests that he has been in love since then, but without success: he has learnt 'keen lessons' that 'love deceives', and whenever he does his mind thinks back to this unsuccessful meeting by the pond. The alliteration of 'wrings with wrong' sounds unpleasant and the venom (partly in the sound, partly in the meaning) of 'God-curst sun' is very bleak and powerful. In artistic terms Hardy brings the poem full circle to end where he began – the pond, the tree, the gray leaves. The pond is stagnant like the relationship, and is part of the pathetic fallacy used through the poem – the dead leaves, the white sun. The landscape is drained of all colour – just as the relationship is drained of all love.

Byron's 'When We Two Parted' is clearly about one individual woman. Hardy's poem is based on a meeting with one individual woman, but he has learnt 'keen lessons that love deceives' since then, which suggests a series of unsuccessful relationships, with the one in 'Neutral Tones' being the first of many. And in what ways can love deceive? Our first thought might be infidelity, but that is not very subtle. Hardy might mean pretending to yourself that you love someone or falling in love with someone before discovering what they are really like or just falling in love with the wrong person. I'm sure you can think of other possibilities. Hardy is claiming that at the end of any relationship he thinks back to this scene by the pond because of its sterile desolation: perhaps it was also the end of his first serious love affair.

Hardy chooses to use a regular rhyme scheme and the poem is made up of four rhyming quatrains written in iambic tetrameter – eight syllables to the line with four stressed syllables. However, Hardy uses enjambment skilfully and there is some metrical variation: 'God-curst sun' consists of three stressed syllables which adds force and power to the words themselves.

In 'Neutral Tones' Hardy

- writes a devastatingly bleak poem about the end of a relationship.

- uses pathetic fallacy in a masterly way to convey the human emotions in the poem.

- writes with a sense of experience about the bitter feelings that relationships can cause.

- apportions no blame for the breakdown of the relationship.

- uses imagery well to convey the sterility of the landscape and by extension the sterility of the relationship.

'My Last Duchess' – Robert Browning

Context

Robert Browning was born in 1812 and became one of the most famous English poets of the Victorian era. He was married to Elizabeth Barrett Browning who was a semi-invalid with an over-protective father. The couple were married in secret and then went to live in Italy. Browning's best work is often set in the past and he was a master of the dramatic monologue, in which the imagined speaker of the poem reveals their innermost thoughts and feelings, often going on to uncover uncomfortable truths about themselves.

This poem is based on real historical events. Duke Alfonso II of Modena and Ferrara (1559 – 1597) married Lucrezia de Doctors and she died four years after the wedding in mysterious circumstances. This is the starting point for Browning's poem. Victorian Britain was rather obsessed with the Italian Renaissance. Many of Browning's monologues are set in Renaissance Italy. The Renaissance, around the period 1450 – 1650, was a cultural and intellectual movement which happened all across Western Europe and it involved the rediscovery of many of the skills that had been forgotten or ignored since the fall of the Roman Empire, especially in painting, art and sculpture. We can understand why the Renaissance began in Italy and the Italians felt themselves to be the heirs of the ancient Romans. In Italy the ruins and ancient buildings were a constant visual reminder of the arts of Rome. The artistic achievement of the Renaissance was helped by a system of patronage: wealthy dukes, merchants and princes commissioned great artists to create paintings and sculptures, just as in the poem the Duke of Ferrara has commissioned Fra Pandolf to paint the portrait of his first wife and Claus of Innsbruck has sculpted Neptune taming a sea-horse.

But the Renaissance, especially in Italy, had a sinister side to it. Many of the wealthy and powerful patrons of art were just as capable of paying to have an enemy assassinated or poisoned because their power and wealth allowed them to do so. What seems to have fascinated the Victorians was the co-existence in the Italian renaissance of art works of stunning beauty alongside moral and political corruption. As Victorian Britons they hoped to emulate the cultural achievements, but looked down upon (even as they were fascinated by) the moral corruption.

Fra Pandolf – an imaginary painter who supposedly painted the portrait of the Duchess.

a day – for many days.

countenance – face.

durst – dared.

mantle – a cloak.

favour – a thing (a jewelled brooch perhaps or a flower) worn as a token of love or affection.

officious – too forward in offering unwelcome or unwanted services.

nine-hundred-years-old name – this simply means that the title the Duke of Ferrara was first created nine-hundred years before the poem is set.

forsooth – truly.

the Count, your master – this phrase is important because it makes clear that the speaker of the poem is talking to a servant of the Count, who is visiting (it later becomes clear) to discuss the marriage of his daughter to the narrator.

munificence – generosity.

nay – no.

Neptune – the God of the Sea.

Claus of Innsbruck – an imaginary sculptor who has sculpted the statue of Neptune for the Duke.

Who? The Duke of Ferrara talks to the representative of an unnamed count who is there to arrange for his daughter to marry the Duke – she will be his next duchess. The poem is written in the present tense.

When? In the 16th century, in the Duke's palace. This is very important because Browning and his fellow Victorians were fascinated by the Italian Renaissance period.

Where? In Ferrara in northern Italy.

What? The speaker tells the story of his first marriage by reference to a portrait of his first wife which hangs on the wall.

Commentary

'My Last Duchess' by Robert Browning is a very famous and much-anthologized poem. It is a dramatic monologue – that is to say the poet adopts the voice of someone else and speaks throughout as that person. It was first published in 1842 and is one of many dramatic monologues that Browning wrote.

The speaker in the poem is the Duke of Ferrara, an Italian nobleman from the 16th century – we are told this from the note at the beginning. This immediately tells us the location of the poem (Italy) and the social background of the speaker – he is a powerful and wealthy aristocrat.

As the poem develops we come to understand that the Duke (pictured here) is talking to a representative of the family of his fiancée, his future wife, and that they are talking in the Duke of Ferrara's palace. We can be even more precise and say that for most of the poem they are standing in front of a portrait of the Duke's former wife (now dead). The Duke talks about his dead wife and, in doing so, reveals a great deal about his character, the sort of man he is. We also learn the terrible fate of his first wife.

The opening sentence refers the reader to a painting hanging on the wall. The painting is so good that his previous wife is

Looking as if she were alive.

Browning establishes that the painter was skilled and produced a *wonder* – a masterpiece. The painter fussed over the portrait and over the duchess – *his hands worked busily a day.* In line 5 we realize for the first time that the duke is speaking not to the readers as such, but someone else; he invites him to sit and look at the portrait of his dead wife. He says he mentioned Fra Pandolf *by design* – perhaps to imply that he was an exceptionally well-known and highly sought-after painter (but remember that he has been made up by Browning). The fact that the Duke could pay for his services shows how rich he is.

The long sentence that begins on line 5 may be a little hard to follow. Note that in lines 9-10 the duke reveals that the painting is normally concealed by a curtain which only he is allowed to open; this suggests, perhaps, a man who is used to being obeyed, even in petty things like a curtain covering a painting. When people like the person he is talking to – *strangers like you* – see the painting, the duke says, they are always moved to ask him (he's always there because he controls the curtain!) what caused the *depth and passion* in the look on the duchess's face. You might note the phrase *its pictured countenance* – I know he is talking about a painted image, but it may strike you as unusual that he doesn't use the word *her* when talking about his dead wife. This one word suggests that he treated her like an object in life and, now that her portrait is on his wall, she is still an object – only now he can exert complete control over her. We might also note that the visitor hasn't asked about the *earnest glance* in the duchess's face – perhaps only the duke sees it. He seems to like the painting of her very much indeed and we will return to this idea later in this commentary.

The duke continues by saying that his visitor is not the first person to ask him why she looked so passionate in the portrait. The duke states

.... Sir, 'twas not

Her husband's presence only, called that spot

Of joy into the Duchess' cheek.

Her husband's presence – are we to assume that he was there in the room all the time while she had her portrait completed? I think we are – it fits with what we are starting to find out about his character. The duke seems to have been jealous when other men paid any attention to his wife – something she appears to have enjoyed since it brings *a spot of joy* to her face. He seems to have seen Fra Pandolf as some sort of rival and repeats things that the painter said to his wife in lines 16 – 19. You may feel that the duke really suspected that Fra Pandolf was his wife's secret lover or you may feel that the duke thought she was a little too easily impressed by male attention.

The duke then expands on his wife's faults. She was *too soon made glad*; she was *too easily impressed*; she could not discriminate –

...she liked whate'er

She looked on and her looks went everywhere.

She looked on everything with the same undiscriminating affection.

My favour at her breast — some precious brooch pinned on her breast and given her by the duke was given the same importance as the sunset or some cherries brought to her by a servant or riding a white mule along the terrace of the palace. You might feel that riding a white mule is a slightly eccentric thing to do — but she is the wife of a wealthy and very powerful man and she can do what she likes, whatever takes her fancy. Above is a picture believed to be of the Duchess that the poem is based upon.

Line 33 reveals the duke's arrogance about his title and position. He talks about his nine-hundred-years-old name and clearly feels that his position and his title as Duke of Ferrara should have been given more respect by his wife. Note that he calls his name *My gift* – as though she should have been grateful that he married her.

In line 34 he starts to suggest that his attitude to all this was casual and relaxed. He calls her behaviour *trifling* and says he would not *stoop* to blame her. *Stoop* is an important word because it reminds us of his high social status and makes it clear that he regarded his wife as beneath him and inferior to him: it is a word that he repeats in the next few lines. And so it was that, even though his wife's behaviour disgusted him, he never said a word.

Browning allows the duke to say he is not good at speaking and so may not have been able to explain his misgivings to his wife – but this is sheer nonsense: every line of this poem shows that the duke (as Browning has created him) is a clever manipulator of words. He says that she might have argued with him: *plainly set her wits* against his; and that even if he could have explained, it would have been degrading for him to have done so

E'en then would be some stooping, and I choose

Never to stoop.

Once again we are reminded of his arrogance and superciliousness. It is interesting that he could not speak to his wife, but he takes 56 lines of the poem to talk to his visitor. She remained friendly to him – she smiled when she passed him, but she smiled at everyone and his sense of his own importance cannot allow that. And then we come to the heart, perhaps, of the poem

... I gave commands;

Then all smiles stopped together.

The duke gave some orders and had his wife murdered. This is quite clear. Browning said of the poem in an interview:

I meant that the commands were that she should be put to death....Or he might have had her shut up in a convent.

Now look back at line 19. It refers to the painter saying that he can never hope to reproduce in paint *the flush that dies along her throat* – that fades along her throat, but now we have read more of the poem and we know what the duke did to his wife, it is clear that Browning is preparing us verbally for the truth. Did she have her throat slashed? Or was she strangled? Either could be true. The flush in line 19 is the way that the Duchess blushed when she was flirting, perhaps, but the fact that Browning uses the verb 'dies' instead of 'fade' is a way of verbally prefiguring her fate. And his final sentence about his wife also suggests that she was murdered: *there she stands/As if alive.*

In line 47 he invites his visitor to stand and go downstairs with him to meet the company – the group of people who are waiting for them down below. Line 49 reveals that he has been talking to a servant of an unnamed Count (*your master*) whose *known munificence* means that he (the duke) expects a very large dowry. Having mentioned the dowry, the duke asserts that he doesn't really care about money – he is only interested in the count's daughter.

As they go down the stairs the duke points out a bronze statue, another of his pieces of art, sculpted by Claus of Innsbruck for him. The statue's subject matter is important: it shows the god of the sea, Neptune, taming a sea-horse. This demonstrates the relationship that the duke had with his first wife (he tamed her), with his servants and with his future wife – the daughter of the Count. Like Neptune ruling the sea, the duke likes to have power over people and beautiful objects like the painting of his wife and this statue. It is significant that the final word of this poem is *me* – because the duke's self-centredness has slowly been revealed the more we have read.

Browning writes in rhyming couplets of ten syllables, but his use of enjambment means that, because the lines are very rarely end-stopped, the poem drives onwards, just as the duke almost compulsively reveals what has happened to his wife. The enjambment also prevents the rhyming couplets from becoming too monotonous and make them sound more like real speech. The duke's hesitations and frequent interjections make him appear reasonable, although he is talking about the murder of his first wife. He has a very casual attitude to it all: he acquired a wife; she did not behave as he liked; he disposed of her. The naturalness of the sound of his speech, its casual, relaxed tone suggests that he does not see anything wrong in what he has done and expects his listener to find it normal too.

Although he claims he is not skilled in speaking, Browning ensures that the Duke gradually reveals the truth about what happened to his wife and the truth about his own character: he is possessive, jealous and likes the idea of controlling people. He is proud and arrogant about his aristocratic title and his family's history. He seems to prefer the painting of his dead wife to her living reality: he can control the painting, but he could not control his first wife. The poem ends on a note of dread – dread on behalf of his second wife who does not know what lies in store for her. He also seems to treat his wives like objects: objects are much easier to control than living human beings.

He seems more interested in being seen as a man of great taste than as a good husband. He draws the servant's attention to the painting and to the sculpture at the end. These objects are meant to demonstrate his taste and his wealth – he is connected to the great artists of his day. But his taste is limited to things he can control and totally possess – for example, he does not seem to be aware of the irony in the sculpture of Neptune and the fact that it might symbolize his relationships with other people, especially women.

Love and Power

The Duke of Ferrara exercises complete power in his palace and its grounds. His power is based on his aristocratic positon – his "nine hundred year old name", his money, and his possessive and jealous personality. There is a paradox here: despite all his money and power, he could not control the behaviour of his wife and – "I gave commands" – he gets rid of his troublesome wife. Now she exists as a painting, covered by curtains which only he can use, so he now has a measure of control over her. His power is also shown by the quick way in which his commands were acted upon and also by his collection of expensive and exquisite works of art. Because this is a dramatic monologue, Browning presents the Duke without comment – in marked contrast to the three preceding Romantic poems where the reader is left in no doubt about the poet's own views. With this poem Browning presents the Duke and allows the reader to make up their own mind about him. This is a poem about love as a means of control and ownership.

Why?

This casual-sounding but deeply sinister poem

- shows the pride and arrogance of the aristocracy.

- is a portrait of the psychology of a murderer.

- shows that money and status and power can corrupt.

- shows the domination of men over women.

- raises questions about the relationship between art and life.

- is superbly written by Browning so that the reader must read between the lines as the terrible truth dawns upon us.

'How Do I Love Thee' – Elizabeth Barrett Browning

Context

Elizabeth Barrett Browning was born into a wealthy family in 1806. At the age of 14 she suffered from a lung complaint and the following year damaged her spine in a riding accident, she was to be plagued with poor health for the rest of her life. Elizabeth had started to publish poetry anonymously and was starting to become famous. In 1838 her brother Edward drowned off the coast of Devon and for the next five years Elizabeth became a recluse, hardly leaving her bedroom in her father's house. However, she continued to write poetry and began a long correspondence with the poet Robert Browning, who began writing to her after reading her poems. Between 1844 and 1846 they wrote 574 letters to each other and finally ran away to Italy to get married. They had to flee to Italy because Elizabeth's father was violently opposed to the marriage. She and her father never spoke again and he disinherited her. Her health improved in Italy and she gave birth to a son in 1849. She died in her husband's arms in 1861.

'Sonnet 43' is from the sonnet cycle *Sonnets from the Portuguese* which she wrote during their correspondence and before their marriage. (*Sonnets from the Portuguese* is simply the title she chose – they are not translations and do not exist in Portuguese!). This sonnet cycle explores the development and growth of her love for Browning and, although she wrote many other poems, it is these sonnets for which she is mainly remembered today. What is interesting and rarely mentioned in guides like this, is that the earlier poems in the sonnet cycle were not as confident as 'Sonnet 43'. In the earlier sonnets she is afraid of the consequences of her love for Browning and unsure about her own feelings: 'Sonnet 43' is towards the end of the sonnet cycle and represents the achievement of a confident, mature love.

Thee- you

Grace – the Grace of God

My lost Saints – perhaps a reference to members of the poet's family who have died or to her former strong religious belief which has been replaced by love for Browning.

Who? The poet addresses her future husband.

When? From the period before they were married.

Where? The location is not specified.

What? The poet explores the many ways in which she loves her husband-to-be.

Commentary

Although this poem is a Petrarchan sonnet in form, it is unlike many sonnets because there is no turn in line 9 – there is no conflict or problem to be resolved because Barrett Browning's tone is assertive, confident and strong: she is expressing her love for Browning without doubt or hesitation.

The opening sentence – given more prominence by the poet's dramatic use of the caesura – asks a question which the following thirteen lines attempt to answer. In all there are eight different aspects of love identified. As the poem goes on each different type of love is introduced by the words *I love thee* – which is a very simple device of repetition, but may explain why so many readers find this a memorable poem. In the first quatrain the poet moves on to speak of the spiritual aspect of her love; the second quatrain deals with the love that enriches ordinary, everyday life. Her love is given *freely* she says in line 7 and *purely* – line 8: her love is given unselfishly and modestly, in the way someone might turn away from praise.

In the sestet the poet analyses her love in three more ways: she loves him with Passion – an emotion she once expended on grief and with the fidelity of a child. She loves him with the same passion she once reserved for religion. She then states that her love is completely overwhelming – it is like breathing and continues through good and bad times – *smiles, tears, of all my life*. The poem ends by stating that if it is God's will, then her love will continue after death and exist in the after-life – another answer to her opening question.

Apart from the lack of a turn or problem to be resolved, which sets it apart from many sonnets, Barrett Browning uses hardly any imagery, no metaphors or similes. She takes an abstract concept 'love' and defines it largely through other abstract concepts – Grace, Right. The words I love thee are repeated nine times in the course of the sonnet and this simple use of repetition has made the poem so well-known and popular. This repetition also shows the strength and confidence of her feelings.

So how does she love her husband?

She loves him with her soul when it is searching for the meaning of life (*the ends of Being*) and the mystery of God (*Ideal Grace*).

She loves him in an ordinary down-to-earth way – *the level of everyday's most quiet need*.

She loves him *freely* – in the same way that humans seek morality (*Right*).

She loves him purely and modestly (*as men turn from Praise*).

She loves him with the passion she once expended on *my old griefs*.

She loves him with the faith of childhood.

She loves him with the love she seemed to lose with her lost Saints (the siblings who had died when she was younger).

She loves him with the breath of all her life.

She will love him better after death.

This famous poem is very simple in its use of language – and perhaps that is its appeal. There are no metaphors to confuse or to analyze; the imagery is limited and where it occurs it is very simple – *sun, candlelight, smiles, tears*; it is clearly written in the Christian tradition and some readers may find her certainty and faith comforting.

Why?

In this famous sonnet, Barratt Browning

- asserts her unequivocal love and fidelity to her husband.
- uses simple language and hardly any imagery.
- expresses complete devotion to her husband.

'1st Date –She & 1st Date – He' – Wendy Cope

Author & Context

Poet Wendy Cope was born in Erith, Kent in 1945 and read History at St Hilda's College, Oxford.

She trained as a teacher at Westminster College of Education, Oxford, and taught in primary schools in London (1967-81 and 1984-6). She became Arts and Reviews editor for *Contact*, the Inner London Education Authority magazine, and continued to teach part-time, before becoming a freelance writer in 1986. She was television critic for *The Spectator* magazine until 1990. She received a Cholmondeley Award in 1987 and was awarded the Michael Braude Award for Light Verse (American Academy of Arts and Letters) in 1995. Her poetry collections include *Making Cocoa for Kingsley Amis* (1986), *Serious Concerns* (1992) and *If I Don't Know* (2001), which was shortlisted for the Whitbread Poetry Award. *Two Cures for Love* (2008) is a selection of previous poems with notes, together with new poems.

She has edited a number of poetry anthologies including *The Orchard Book of Funny Poems* (1993), *Is That The New Moon?* (1989), *The Funny Side: 101 Humorous Poems* (1998) and *The Faber Book of Bedtime Stories* (1999) and *Heaven on Earth: 101 Happy Poems* (2001). She is also the author of two books for children, *Twiddling Your Thumbs* (1988) and *The River Girl* (1991). Wendy Cope is a Fellow of the Royal Society of Literature and lives in Winchester, England. In 1998 she was the listeners' choice in a BBC Radio 4 poll to succeed Ted Hughes as Poet Laureate.

Her latest collection is *Family Values* (2011). She was awarded an OBE in 2010.

besotted – infatuated by, obsessed by, when applied to love.

Who? Two people who are going on their first date together.

When? Evening.

Where? A classical music concert hall.

What? Cope cleverly gives two accounts of the same experience from two different points of view. Both speakers seem lacking in confidence and anxious to create a good impression on their first date: this leads to some amusing misunderstandings.

Commentary

This comic poem has an unusual arrangement, because it is split into two columns, the first entitled 'Ist Date -She' and the second 'Ist Date – He' This enables Cope to give the two speakers their different thoughts on the date and what is going on.

The first funny thing for me is that neither of them are very keen on classical music, but they are both attending a classical music concert.

The woman says:

I said I liked classical music.

It wasn't exactly a lie.

I hoped he would get the impression

That my brow was acceptably high.

In other words, she says she likes classical music to impress him. He is similar in his self-delusion, saying *I implied I was keen on it too*, but he admits that although he rarely attends concerts *It wasn't entirely untrue*, which really means it is partly untrue.

In her second verse the woman writes that she mentioned *Vivaldi and Bach* and *he asked me along to this concert*. The man in his second verse reveals that he *looked for a suitable concert, / And here we are on our first date* – a date neither of them want to be on really given their minimal interest in classical music. They are attracted to each other and the concert is just a badly-chosen first date based on minor deception. The man is more concerned that the traffic that evening was *dreadful* and that he was *ten minutes late.*

In the woman's third stanza she admits that she was thrilled to be asked to the concert, but she couldn't care less what they play. Her attention is really on her date, the man she is attracted to, not the music at all:

But I'm trying my hardest to listen

So I'll have something clever to say.

This deeply ironic – the man knows very little about classical music and would not recognize if she had something clever to say or not.

Going to a concert on a first date is not a good idea because there are few opportunities to talk and get to know each other. In his third stanza the man looks at the woman's face and comes to the completely, laughably wrong conclusion:

She is totally lost in the music

And quite undistracted by me.

Cope then follows this with the woman's fourth stanza – which is hilarious given the man's observations:

When I glance at his face it's a picture

Of rapt concentration. I see

He is totally into this music

And quite undistracted by me.

This is funny partly because it echoes exactly the man's words, partly because, like the man's observation it is completely untrue and partly because the exact opposite is true – the man is attracted to her as his fourth stanza reveals.

The man's fourth stanza begins with his real interest – *In that dress she is very attractive* – and the second line refers admiringly to her neckline. However, as he has admitted in the third verse, he is a bit nervous and now, in stanza four, he tells himself

I mustn't appear too besotted.

Perhaps she is out of my league.

Clearly he IS besotted with her as a woman, but is held back, perhaps, by a lack of self-confidence and a fear of rejection… and, of course, by the formality of a classical music concert hall where they cannot speak to each other.

In the man's fifth stanza (the ninth stanza of the poem as a whole), he is unsure where they are in the programme of music: he does have a physical programme but has put his reading glasses away. He says to himself:

I'd better start paying attention

Or else I'll have nothing to say.

This is richly ironic because in her third stanza the woman had told herself to listen harder so that she would have something clever to say; she clearly wants to impress the man with her cleverness.

The poem as a whole presents a very funny situation: a man and a woman who are attracted to each other, but have not got the nerve to admit it, attend a classical music concert as a first date. They want to impress each other by having something to say about the concert, but they both misinterpret what the other is thinking. They are both thinking about each other, but, comically, each one is convinced that they are concentrating on the concert when nothing could be further from the truth. Although the poem is funny and highly ironic, there is a serious side, showing how difficult it is sometimes for would-be lovers to communicate their real feelings. The real joke is that neither of the speakers really wants to be at the concert at all and neither of them have any particular interest in classical music – they are much more interested in each other, but too wary to admit it and too keen to make a good impression.

Why?

In this amusing poem Wendy Cope:

- uses irony throughout by using dual narrators.
- shows both speakers to be reticent about what they really want to do.
- hints at a certain sadness because the would-be lovers are too self-conscious to be true to themselves.

'Valentine' – Carol Ann Duffy

Author & Context

Dame Carol Ann Duffy DBE FRSL (born 23 December 1955) is a Scottish poet and playwright. She is Professor of Contemporary Poetry at Manchester Metropolitan University, and was appointed Britain's Poet Laureate in May 2009. She is the first woman, the first Scot, and the first openly LGBT person to hold the position. Her collections include *Standing Female Nude* (1985), winner of a Scottish Arts Council Award; *Selling Manhattan* (1987), which won a Somerset Maugham Award; *Mean Time* (1993), which won the Whitbread Poetry Award; and *Rapture* (2005), winner of the T. S. Eliot Prize. Her poems address issues such as oppression, gender, and violence in an accessible language that has made them popular in schools.

Commentary

When we think of a Valentine's Day gift, our minds are apt to turn to clichés: red roses, chocolates, fancy lingerie, soft toys (usually teddy bears) holding little hearts – the conventional approach to Valentine's Day. Duffy dismisses all this tat in the first single-line stanza of her poem 'Valentine'.

Not a red rose or a satin heart.

Her gift for her lover is very different:

I give you an onion.

This is shocking, unsettling and funny at the same time.

She then uses a metaphor to describe the onion *as a moon wrapped in brown paper.* It has to be unpeeled and its unpeeling is like the way we unpeel our clothes as we prepare for sex. The moon is also a romantic image commonly associated with love, but this one comes wrapped in unromantic brown paper, Duffy again eschewing any of the romantic clichés of Valentine's Day.

Cutting onions makes you cry and Duffy goes on to promise that this onion will make her lover cry. Tears are associated with love in two ways: they can be tears of happiness and ecstasy or they can be tears of grief and sadness when love goes wrong or there are difficulties in the relationship. Duffy's onion offers both.

The next stanza certainly suggests there are problems in the relationship. Her lover will be *blinded by tears* and her reflection will become *a wobbling photo of grief.*

Duffy admits she is being *truthful* and again rejects the *cute card[s] and kissograms* of the conventional Valentine's Day celebrations.

Duffy claims that the onions

... fierce kiss, will stay on your lips,

Possessive and faithful

As we are,

For as long as we are.

The pungent aroma of the onion and its *fierce kiss* (indicative of fierce sexual passion) will always be on her lips – *for as long as we are*: for as long as their relationship continues.

In the final stanza Duffy is still urging her lover to accept the onion: *Take it.* The circular hoops of the onion get smaller and smaller and are white and

Its platinum hoops shrink to a wedding ring

If you like.

But Duffy's one-word line following this – *Lethal* – suggests she views marriage in a negative light, perhaps lethal to a relationship based on love. Certainly the earlier *for as long as we are* assumed that the relationship would one day come to an end.

Love, Duffy writes, as an onion *will cling to your fingers* – like the odours of sexual activity cling to one's fingers – and they will *cling to your knife* – an especially threatening way to end the poem, as if not only do you use a knife to cut an onion, but you might use it to break a relationship. Love can be a dangerous emotion if it is not returned.

Duffy's tone throughout the poem is scathing about the conventional rituals of Valentine's Day – and probably rightly so. Her use of single line stanzas, short sentences and simple vocabulary adds a harshness and honesty to her words. Elsewhere her brevity and the general shortness of her phrases suggests an honesty and no-nonsense approach to love – softened at points when she mentions the platinum wedding ring, only to dismiss it as *lethal*. Is she suggesting that marriage destroys love?

She conveys the reality of love – the tears of joy and happiness or of sadness and heartbreak. Above all, she delights and surprises the reader with her gift of an onion.

Why?

In 'Valentine' Carol Ann Duffy

- rejects the traditional symbols of romantic love.
- offers an onion as a Valentine's Day gift – and goes on to explain why it is an appropriate gift.

- shows how love can lead to heartbreak and tears when it goes wrong.
- shocks and amuses the reader by her choice of an onion.
- strongly suggests that marriage can result in the loss of love.

'One Flesh' – Elizabeth Jennings

Author and Context

Jennings was born in Boston, Lincolnshire. When she was six, her family moved to Oxford, where she remained for the rest of her life. There she later attended St Anne's College. After graduation, she became a writer.

Jennings' early poetry was published in journals such as *Oxford Poetry*, *New English Weekly*, *The Spectator*, *Outposts* and *Poetry Review*, but her first book was not published until she was 27. The lyrical poets she cited as having influenced her were Hopkins, Auden, Graves and Muir. Her second book, *A Way of Looking*, won the Somerset Maugham award and marked a turning point, as the prize money allowed her to spend nearly three months in Rome, which was a revelation. It brought a new dimension to her religious belief and inspired her imagination.

Regarded as traditionalist rather than an innovator, Jennings is known for her lyric poetry and mastery of form. Her work displays a simplicity of metre and rhyme shared with Philip Larkin, Kingsley Amis and Thom Gunn, all members of the group of English poets known as The Movement. She always made it clear that, whilst her life, which included a spell of severe mental illness, contributed to the themes contained within her work, she did not write explicitly autobiographical poetry. Her deeply held Roman Catholicism coloured much of her work.

She died in a care home in Bampton, Oxfordshire and is buried in Wolvercote Cemetery, Oxford.

flotsam - the wreckage of a ship or its cargo found floating on or washed up by the sea.

Who? The poet writes about her elderly parents who occupy the central place in the poem.

Where? In bed.

When? In the old age of Elizabeth Jennings' parents.

What? Jennings speculates about the state of their marriage now they are elderly and their youthful passion has disappeared.

Commentary

This poem is arranged in three stanzas, reflecting the three people in the poem: the poet, her father and her mother. Jennings uses a strict rhyme scheme which helps to show that her feelings, although deep, are restrained and under control – just as the language is under control. Each stanza follows the same rhyme scheme with some half-rhymes: ABABAA, although there is some variation in the last verse, which is ABABAB and does contain some half-rhyme.

The opening stanza is descriptive and reflective. Her parents are in bed – separate beds – and her father has a book, keeping the light on late. Her mother, by contrast, is

> ... *like a girl dreaming of childhood,*
>
> *All men elsewhere.*

Jennings feels that

> ... *it is as if they wait*
>
> *Some new event: the book he holds unread,*
>
> *Her eyes fixed on the shadows overhead.*

But no new event is likely given their age and state. All that awaits them is death.

The second stanza begins with a simile – her parents are *Tosssed up like flotsam from a former passion,* but now the passion has disappeared and they *lie cool.* We are told that they *hardly ever touch* and if they ever do

> ... *it is like a confession*

Of having little feeling – or too much.

This is a deliberate paradox: perhaps they hardly ever touch because their feelings for each other have faded and withered; but perhaps they hardly ever touch because to do so is to recall their youthful, passionate days which are long gone – and it is painful to think about the past now they are old and decrepit.

The third stanza begins with a paradox they are *Strangely apart, yet strangely close together* – joined by their daughter and by decades of married life. They no longer talk much but the silence between them is *like a thread to hold* but *not wind in*: they are connected and perhaps content with the silence but it does not bring them closer together. Jennings then uses a very interesting metaphor:

And time itself's a feather

Touching them gently.

This is a beautiful and delicate image which suggests the frailty of old age and the gentleness with which they are touched by time; it may also refer directly to the physical frailty they both endure. Time has to be gentle with them.

In the final sentence Jennings asks a rhetorical question which reveals the real concern of the poem:

Do they know they're old,

These two who are my father and my mother

Whose fire from which I came, has now grown cold?

Here the contrast between the youthful passion they felt in their younger years has grown cold. Therefore, a poem which has a morose and melancholic tone throughout becomes a lament on the inevitable process of ageing and the loss of youthful vigour and energy.

Why?

In 'One Flesh' Elizabeth Jennings

- speculates on the state of her parents' marriage now that they are very old.
- presents her parents as almost leading separate lives in one house.
- speculates on the youthful passion that led to Jennings' birth and wonders what they have now to replace it.
- writes a rather melancholic poem, the tone of which is subdued and morose.

'i wanna be yours' – John Cooper Clarke

Author & Context

John Cooper Clarke (born 25 January 1949) is an English performance poet who first became famous during the punk rock era of the late 1970s when he became known as a "punk poet". He released several albums in the late 1970s and early 1980s, and continues to perform regularly. His recorded output has mainly centred on musical backing from the Invisible Girls, which featured Martin Hannett, Steve Hopkins, Pete Shelley, Bill Nelson, and Paul Burgess.

Commentary

John Cooper Clarke is a performance poet and I would strongly recommend that you watch some of his performances on Youtube before you read the commentary that follows.

'i wanna be yours' is a funny poem, even funnier, I would suggest, in performance. It relies on repetition, simple rhymes and unusual metaphors for its comic effect. The opening is typical of the whole poem:

let me be your vacuum cleaner

breathing in your dust

let me be your ford cortina

i will never rust

The humour here is two-fold. Firstly, everyday objects like vacuum cleaners and Ford Cortinas do not often appear in love poems – so there is the shock of the bizarre and the unusual. Secondly, while love poetry is full of poets offering to perform actions for their loved ones, the thought of a human being transformed to a vacuum cleaner or a type of car borders on the surreal.

The second half of the first stanza continues in similar vein:

if you like your coffee hot

let me be your coffee pot

you call the shots

i wanna be yours

The last two lines are slightly shorter than the others and break the pattern of the previous six.

In the second stanza he offers to be her raincoat, her dreamboat and her teddy bear which she can

take… with you anywhere

i don't care

i wanna be yours

The metrical pattern of the second verse is exactly the same as the first and the effects are just as amusing.

The third stanza begins as the first two do with surreal offers to prove his love and devotion:

let me be your electric meter

i will not run out

let me be your electric heater

you get cold without

He then expresses a desire to be her setting lotion and this starts a riff on words that rhyme with lotion: he will hold her hair

with deep devotion

deep as the deep

atlantic ocean

that's how deep is my devotion

deep deep deep deep de deep deep

i don't wanna be hers

i wanna be yours

Throughout the poem Cooper Clarke uses simple vocabulary to convey straightforward emotions in a funny and engaging style.

Why?

In this funny performance poem John Cooper Clarke

- rejects the traditional clichés of romantic love.
- uses everyday language and objects in interesting, amusing and new ways.
- expresses complete devotion and love in a humorous way.

'Love's Dog' – Jen Hatfield

Author & Context

Jen Hadfield was born in Cheshire, England, to Canadian and British parents. She earned her BA from the University of Edinburgh and MLitt in creative writing from the University of Strathclyde and the University of Glasgow, where she worked with the poet Tom Leonard. Hadfield's first collection, *Almanacs* (2005), explored Canadian and Scottish topography, in particular the Shetland Islands where Hadfield still lives, paying special attention to how dialects and local languages emerge from landscapes, labour, and encounters with other cultures. For her second book, *Nigh-No-Place* (2008), Hadfield won a T.S. Eliot Prize, making her the youngest poet ever to do so. Of both books Hadfield has written, "the poems are united by my fascination with spoken language and by themes of wildness and subsistence; fretting over what it means to be 'no-place' and what it means to make yourself 'at home.'"

Hadfield is also a visual artist and bookmaker. In 2007, she received a DeWar Award to travel to Mexico and study Mexican devotional folk art. She is a member of the artists' collective Veer North and provided photographs for the collaborative artists' book *The Printer's Devil and the Little Bear* (2006). Hadfield's honours and awards include an Eric Gregory Award, a Scottish Arts Council Bursary Award, and residencies with the Shetland Arts Trust and the Scottish Poetry Library. In 2014, she was named one of 20 poets selected to represent the Next Generation of UK poets. Hadfield currently lives in the Shetland Islands, where she is reader in residence at Shetland Library.

The poem was inspired by 'A View of Things' by the Scottish poet Edwin Morgan which contains the line *What I hate about love is its dog.*

Who? There is one speaker, probably the poet.

When? No specific time is mentioned.

Where? There is no specific location.

What? The poem is a list of the things the poet loves and hates about love.

Commentary

This is an anaphoric poem – that is to say that the lines begin with the same words (with some variations). Generally, in this poem each line begins *What I love about love is its...*, although *hate* and *loathe* are used to replace *love*. The poem consists of eight two line stanzas with occasional rhyme and half-rhyme. I think this poem would cause laughter at a poetry reading and I hope to explain why.

The first verse makes perfect sense

What I love about love is its diagnosis

What I hate about love is its prognosis

The *diagnosis* may well refer to the fact and realization that you are in love, while the *prognosis* may refer to the future of the relationship and a possible future break up.

Usually the words at the end of the line relate to each other in one way or another, as in stanza three

What I love about love is its petting zoo

What I love about love is its zookeeper – you

From this point on in the poem the things mentioned are increasingly random, as in the fifth stanza:

What I love about love is its doubloons

What I love about love is its bird-bones.

In the following stanza she hates love's boilwash, but loves its spin cycle: these domestic details are bizarre and random, and the poem is deliberately and playfully descending into nonsense. There is a long tradition of nonsense verse in English Literature.

The penultimate stanza is wholly negative:

What I loathe about love is its burnt toast and bonemeal

What I hate about love is its bent cigarette

These domestic details keep the poem grounded in reality, but their yoking together at the end of the lines introduces a surreal element — which is true of all the line endings.

The final stanza continues this surreal and amusing tone:

What I love about love is its pirate

What I hate about love is its sick parrot

An amusing and bizarre end to this funny poem. The humour lies at the end of the lines where disparate objects are joined together or juxtaposed. In addition, the objects singled out have very little to do with traditional images of love. Only in stanza three does Hatfield admit to another person to whom these lines are addressed.

Why?

In 'Love's Dog' Jen Hatfield

- writes a funny poem by juxtaposing unusual things, not normally associated with love.
- the poem is given structure by its anaphoric nature.
- creates humour through the often bizarre juxtaposition of things at the end of each line.
- acts as a homage to Edwin Morgan whose line inspired the poem.

'Nettles' – Vernon Scannell

Author & Context

Vernon Scannell (1922 – 2007) was born in Spilsby in Lincolnshire and led a very interesting life, working as both a teacher and a boxer before becoming a full-time writer. The defining experience of his life was being a soldier in the British Army in the Second World War. He fought in North Africa and took part in the 1944 invasion of Normandy, during which he was wounded. Time and time again in his poetry he returns to the war and his memories of it and how they have altered his life.

nettle bed – an area of neglected land on which lots of nettles grow.

hook – scythe, for chopping down tall plants.

Who? Scannell, his son and the mother (*us* in line eight)

When? When Scannell's son was three.

Where? In the back garden, behind the shed where the nettles grow.

What? The poet's son has fallen in the nettle bed and runs to his parents for comfort. His parents soothe him and then Scannell takes his scythe and cuts the nettles down, before burning them. In two weeks they have grown again.

Commentary

In this poem Scannell explores his feelings of care, gentleness and compassion for his son, taking an incident from his son's childhood as a starting point, it reflects on the relationship between father and son. It is tightly structured in rhyming quatrains, but Scannell uses enjambment extensively to make the poem sound almost like real speech and to draw attention away from the rhyme scheme – except at the very start and end of the poem where he uses end-stopped lines.

The blunt opening line, expressed in very simple language, tells us all we need to know about the situation:

My son aged three fell in the nettle bed.

This simple statement of fact is then followed by a detailed description of the incident. Scannell then reflects on how inappropriate that word *bed* is for something which causes so much pain. Bed is a place where we rest, but his son is clearly very distressed – he rushes to his parents in sobs and tears and Scannell sees *blisters beaded* on his son's skin. His pain is raw and after a while he has *a watery grin* – he is grinning through the tears. Scannell's reaction then is one of rage and protective anger. He hacks the nettles down – *slashed in fury* – and then burns the nettles in order that his son will not be hurt again. Scannell makes extensive use of alliteration, especially sibilance, to emphasise the strong feelings which this incident provoked as well as strong and vivid verbs like *slashed* and words like *fury* and *fierce*.

Scannell uses an extended metaphor to describe the nettles in military terms, suggesting he has had first-hand experience of warfare and that the nettles are violent and aggressive and opposed to human life: *spears, regiment, parade, the fallen dead, recruits.* This metaphor also personifies the nettles (even the word *pyre* is normally associated with humans), but Scannell also personifies *the busy sun and rain* who in two weeks had *called up tall recruits behind the shed* – more nettles which may hurt his son. The final line is full of foreboding and, like the opening line, makes complete sense on its own:

My son would often feel sharp wounds again.

It is tempting, isn't it, to see in this line not just a warning about the nettles behind the shed which have grown back so quickly, but a warning about the future in general. Then the poem becomes something else: it is grounded in a clearly remembered event from his son's childhood, but it is a lament for the human condition – just by being alive, Scannell's son will feel sharp wounds again. You might be tempted to go even further and see the military imagery used about the nettles as a warning of what happens to young men in wars – they die – and Scannell knew this from his own experience in the Second World War. Nature too is very hostile in this poem (it isn't in all the poems in the Anthology): the nettles are obviously dangerous and cause pain, but they are helped to grow by the sun and the rain. And what about the bed? Bed is a place of rest, but it can also be the place where you die.

Why?

This poem, based on an everyday incident:

- is a moving poem about a father's love for his son.

- is a warning about his son's future suffering and regrets that the father will not be able to protect his son forever.

- nature is seen as hostile and threatening to human welfare.

- suffering is an inevitable part of being human.

- future wars will also cause pain and suffering.

'The Manhunt' (Laura's Poem) – Simon Armitage

Context

Simon Armitage was born in 1963 in the village of Marsden in West Yorkshire and has spent most of his life in that area. He is a very successful and highly-regarded poet, celebrated for his down-to-earth language and subject matter. Several of his poems are in the Anthology. His poetry often (but not always) deals with the ordinary incidents and events of modern life and appear to be based on personal experience. '

This poem was originally written for a television documentary (Channel 4 – *Forgotten Heroes: The Not Dead*) about soldiers who live with the long-term effects of being involved in warfare and suffering from post-traumatic stress syndrome. In the documentary the poem is read by Laura Beddoes, whose husband Eddie had served as a peace-keeper with the British Army in Bosnia. For this reason, the poem is sometimes called 'Manhunt: Laura's Story'. Eddie was discharged because of injury and depression and the poem explores the impact this had on his marriage. Armitage listened to many accounts by soldiers of their experiences in order to get the inspiration for this poem. He has said:

Never having been to the front line, turning the words, phrases and experiences of these soldiers into verse has been the closest I've ever come to writing 'real' war poetry, and as close as I ever want to get.

Bosnia was once part of Yugoslavia. When the Communist system all over Eastern Europe fell, in Yugoslavia ethnic and religious tensions which had been controlled and suppressed under communism came to the surface. By the mid-1990s the different ethnic groups began fighting each other and committing acts of genocide. The United Kingdom and other NATO countries responded by sending troops to the region to act as peace-keepers and to keep the warring factions apart. In particular, they were attempting to protect Bosnia from attacks by its more powerful neighbour – Serbia.

Who? Armitage adopts the voice of Laura who narrates the poem in the past tense.

When? After Eddie has returned injured, physically and mentally, from war.

Where? No specific location.

What? Laura explains how she very slowly re-discovered the man that Eddie had become.

Commentary

This poem is written in free verse with frequent use of rhyme and half-rhyme. On the page it is divided into separate two line couplets but the lines are of unequal length. This immediately suggests that it looks like a normal poem but it isn't. In the poem we will find that Eddie's mental wounds are much worse than his physical ones – so he may look normal but underneath the surface he is suffering a terrible trauma because of what he has seen in war. Note the deliberate ambiguity of the title: if you are looking for an escaped soldier or airman you 'launch a manhunt'. Laura is on a manhunt but for the man she used to know before he went to war.

The repetition of *then* and *and* is very important in the poem: it suggests that each step in renewing her love for Eddie, in trying to find him again, in trying to understand what he had suffered, is a step in a very slow process. They quickly re-establish a physical relationship with

... passionate nights and intimate days

And she then starts to explore his physical wounds by touching his wounds and scars. In these lines the human body's fragility is emphasized in the metaphors – *porcelain collar-bone, parachute silk* – and his body is seen in terms of machines which do not quite work - *broken hinge, fractured rudder.* In some ways these images are re-assuring because broken hinges can be fixed.

But line 16 mentions Eddie's *grazed heart* and the rest of the poem becomes more difficult in the sense that his mental wounds are invisible and more permanent. Does his *grazed heart* suggest he has lost the ability to love? The fragments left by the bullet are a *metal foetus* – a metaphor that suggests something is growing inside him. Laura then widened the search (remember she is still on a manhunt for the man she used to know) – and finds

... a sweating, unexploded mine

buried deep in his mind, around which

every nerve in his body had tightened and closed.

And this confirms that what really makes Eddie so distant is his mental trauma at the sights and sounds of war, the suffering he witnessed that he now cannot forget. And

Then, and only then, did I come close.

And so the poem ends with the manhunt unsuccessful: Laura does not find him – she only comes close. And comes close to what? The man that Eddie now is? An understanding of what he has been through? What he has seen and heard in Bosnia?

Armitage gives Laura a voice of incredible sensitivity and feeling in this poem. She remains loyal to her lover, despite the difficulty she has in renewing her relationship with him. Eddie remains throughout the poem passive, silent and unknown – which actually makes his mental torments more terrible because they remain hidden and unknown, perhaps unknowable.

This contemporary poem raises with powerful sensitivity

- the long-term effects of warfare on soldiers and their loved ones.
- how the human mind can cope with images and memories of suffering.

- the traumatizing mental scars that ex-soldiers carry with them and which affect their relationships.

'My Father Would Not Show Us' – Ingrid de Kok

Author & Context

Ingrid de Kok grew up in Stilfontein, a gold mining town in what was then the Western Transvaal. When she was 12 years old, her parents moved to Johannesburg. In 1977 she emigrated to Canada where she lived until returning to South Africa in 1984. She has one child, a son. Her partner is Tony Morphet. Ingrid is a Fellow of the University of Cape Town, an Associate Professor in Extra Mural Studies and part of a team of two that designs and administers the public non-formal educational curriculum that constitutes the Extra-Mural Programmes at the University of Cape Town. She has also designed and co-ordinated national colloquiums and cultural programmes, such as one on Technology and Reconstruction and on Equal Opportunity Policy and At the Fault Line: Cultural Inquiries into Truth and Reconciliation and runs various capacity building, civic and trade union programmes. She alternates in the role of Director.

She has acted as a consultant for various adult educational courses or events, (for example, for writers' seminars, cultural forums, and Northwestern University and the University of Chicago's Study Abroad programmes). She has also co-ordinated schools and public programmes devoted to the development of a reading culture. She is a member of PEN, South Africa and a Trustee of Buchu Publishing Project. She was a member of the committee of the National Arts Festival in Grahamstown, South Africa with responsibility for convening the Winter School from 2000 - 2005 and is currently on the National Arts Council Literary Advisory Committee. She is the Chair of the South African Association of Canadian Studies.

Between 1977 and 2006 Ingrid's poems have been published in numerous South African literary journals, including *Upstream*, *Sesame*, *Staffrider*, *Contrast*, *New* Contrast, *New Coin*, Carapace. Occasionally poems have also appeared, translated into Afrikaans, in various South African Afrikaans newspapers.

counterpane – a bed cover.

Who? The poet speaks for herself about her father's death. She has siblings.

When? After her father's death.

Where? At the undertakers and at the family house.

What? De Kok laments her father's death and reflects on what he was like when he was alive.

Commentary

The poem begins with an epigraph by the German poet Rilke: *Which way do we face to talk to the dead?* suggesting perhaps that De Kok wants to talk to her dead father, but now she cannot – except in this poem. The poem is organised into seven stanzas and is written in free verse, although De Kok uses some rhyme towards the end of the poem which suggests a resolution of her feelings.

In the first stanza she visits the undertaker's to see her father's corpse. He has been dead for five days. His face *is organised for me to see* – which suggests a certain artificiality. The second stanza continues with this sense of artificiality: the room is cold (to stop the body decaying) and the *borrowed coffin* he is lying in *gleams unnaturally*. He will be buried in a cheaper pine coffin.

The poet is clearly at the head of the coffin looking down its length which is why her father's face is inverted. She had not expected to see him wearing

...the soft, for some

reason unfrozen collar of his striped pyjamas.

The sight of his pyjamas leads to a stanza of reflection on her childhood. The fourth stanza begins:

This is the last time I am allowed

To remember my childhood as it might have been.

The key words here are *as it might have been*: what follows is not a description of her childhood as it actually was, but as it might have been had her father been a different man. De Kok imagines her home as

a louder, braver place,

crowded, a house with a tin roof

being hailed upon, and voices rising,

my father's wry smile, his half-turned face.

But this is not what her childhood was like. Far from being loud and brave, her father was taciturn and distant as the opening to the next stanza suggests: *My father would not show us how to die* – just as he has not shown them many things. Faced with the fact of dying her father *hid, he hid away / behind the curtains where his life had been... he lay inside he lay.* De Kok's father's reticence extends to the fact of his dying: perhaps he wants to protect his family; perhaps he wants to show courage and stoicism in the face of death.

The next stanza deals with things he remembers on his death bed. His memory of his childhood is very clear:

He could recall the rag-and-bone man

passing his mother's gate in the morning light.

now the tunnelling sounds of the dogs next door....

Towards the end of life, we begin to lose our faculties and her father can no longer hear properly: *everything he hears is white* – a complete blank.

The final stanza begins with a subtle change of word: *My father could not show us how to die* [My emboldening]. Perhaps he could not show them how to die, because he does not know himself. We face death alone – even if we are surrounded by family and friends, we have to face the final days knowing the inevitable will come. De Kok's father retreats from his family as if to protect them from his death:

He turned, he turned away.

Under the counterpane, without one call

or word or name,

face to the wall he lay.

He dies alone which is tribute to his courage and stoicism, but also to protect his family from the fact of death. He is isolated in death and we get a sense of De Kok's sorrow in the repeated *turned away* in the final stanza.

Why?

In this poem Ingrid De Kok

- presents a lament for the death of her father.

- the epigraph suggests there are still things she would like to talk to him about.

- the poem presents her father as a reticent and taciturn man, not used to expressing emotions.

- her father also shows great courage and selflessness in facing death alone.

Glossary

The Oxford Concise Dictionary of Literary Terms has been invaluable in writing this section of the book. I would again remind the reader that knowledge of these terms is only the start – do NOT define a word you find here in the examination. You can take it for granted that the examiner knows the term: it is up to you to try to use it confidently and with precision and to explain why the poet uses it or what effect it has on the reader.

ALLITERATION   the repetition of the same sounds – usually initial consonants or stressed syllables – in any sequence of closely adjacent words.

ALLUSION   an indirect or passing reference to some event, person, place or artistic work which is not explained by the writer, but which relies on the reader's familiarity with it.

AMBIGUITY   openness to different interpretations.

ANAPHORA   In writing or speech, the deliberate repetition of the first part of the sentence in order to achieve an artistic effect is known as Anaphora.

ASSONANCE   the repetition of similar vowel sounds in neighbouring words.

BALLAD   a folk song or orally transmitted poem telling in a simple and direct way a story with a tragic ending. Ballads are normally composed in quatrains with the second and fourth lines rhyming. Such quatrains are known as the ballad stanza because of its frequent use in what we call ballads.

BLANK VERSE   unrhymed lines of ten syllable length. This is a widely used form by Shakespeare in his plays, by Milton and by Wordsworth.

CAESURA   any pause in a line of verse caused by punctuation. This can draw attention to what precedes or follows the caesura and also, by breaking up the rhythm of the line, can slow the poem down and make it more like ordinary speech.

CANON   a body of writings recognized by authority. The canon of a national literature is a body of writings especially approved by critics or anthologists and deemed suitable for academic study. Towards the end of the 20th century there was a general feeling that the canon of English Literature was dominated by dead white men and since then there has been a deliberate and fruitful attempt made to give more prominence to writing by women and by writers from non-white backgrounds. Even your Anthology is a contribution to the canon, because someone sat down and decided that the poems included in it were worthy of study by students taking GCSE.

CARPE DIEM   a Latin phrase from the Roman poet Horace which means 'seize the day' – 'make the best of the present moment'. It is a very common theme of European lyric poetry, in which the speaker of a poem argues that since time is short and death is inevitable, pleasure should be enjoyed while there is still time.

COLLOCATION   the act of putting two words together. What this means in practice is that certain words have very common collocations – in other words they are usually found in written or spoken English in collocation with other words. For example, the word *Christmas* is often collocated with words such as *cards, presents, carols, holidays,* but you won't often find it collocated with *sadness.* This can be an important term because poets, who are seeking to use words in original ways, will often put two words together which are not often collocated.

COLLOQUIALISM   the use of informal expressions or vocabulary appropriate to everyday speech rather than the formality of writing. When used in poetry it can make the poem seem more down-to-earth and real, more honest and intimate.

CONCEIT   an unusually far-fetched metaphor presenting a surprising and witty parallel between two apparently dissimilar things or feelings.

CONSONANCE   the repetition of identical or similar consonants in neighbouring words whose vowel sounds are different.

CONTEXT   the biographical, social, cultural and historical circumstances in which a text is produced and read and understood – you might like to think of it as its background. However, it is important sometimes to consider the reader's own context – especially when we look back at poems from the Literary Heritage. To interpret a poem with full regard to its background is to contextualize it.

COUPLET   a pair of rhyming verse lines, usually of the same length.

CROSSED RHYME the rhyming of one word in the middle of a long line of poetry with a word in a similar position in the next line.

DIALECT a distinctive variety of language, spoken by members of an identifiable regional group, nation or social class. Dialects differ from one another in pronunciation, vocabulary and grammar. Traditionally they have been looked down on and viewed as variations from an educated 'standard' form of the language, but linguists point out that standard forms themselves are merely dialects which have come to dominate for social and political reasons. In English this notion of dialect is especially important because English is spoken all over the world and there are variations between the English spoken in, say, Yorkshire, Delhi and Australia. Dialects now are increasingly celebrated as a distinct way of speaking and writing which are integral to our identity.

DICTION the choice of words used in any literary work.

DISSONANCE harshness of sound.

DRAMATIC MONOLOGUE a kind of poem in which a single fictional or historical character (not the poet) speaks to a silent audience and unwittingly reveals the truth about their character.

ELEGY a lyric poem lamenting the death of a friend or public figure or reflecting seriously on a serious subject. The elegiac has come to refer to the mournful mood of such poems.

ELLIPSIS — the omission from a sentence of a word or words which would be required for complete clarity. It is used all the time in everyday speech, but is often used in poetry to promote compression and/or ambiguity. The adjective is elliptical.

END-RHYME — rhyme occurring at the end of a line of poetry. The most common form of rhyme.

END-STOPPED — a line of poetry brought to a pause by the use of punctuation. The opposite of enjambment.

ENJAMBMENT — caused by the lack of punctuation at the end of a line of poetry, this causes the sense (and the voice when the poem is read aloud) to 'run over' into the next line. In general, this can impart to poems the feel of ordinary speech, but there are examples in the Anthology of more precise reasons for the poet to use enjambment.

EPIPHANY — a sudden moment of insight or revelation, usually at the end of a poem.

EPIZEUXIS — the technique by which a word is repeated for emphasis with no other words intervening

EUPHONY — a pleasing smoothness of sound

FALLING RHYTHM — the effect produced by several lines in succession which end with a feminine ending

FEMININE ENDING — the ending of a line of poetry on an unstressed syllable

FIGURATIVE — Not literal. Obviously 'figurative' language

covers metaphor and simile and personification

FIGURE OF SPEECH   any expression which departs from the ordinary literal sense or normal order of words. Figurative language (the opposite of literal language) includes metaphor, simile and personification. Some figures of speech – such as alliteration and assonance achieve their effects through the repetition of sounds.

FOREGROUNDING   giving unusual prominence to one part of a text. Poetry differs from everyday speech and prose by its use of regular rhythm, metaphors, alliteration and other devices by which its language draws attention to itself.

FREE VERSE   a kind of poetry that does not conform to any regular pattern of line length or rhyme. The length of its lines are irregular as is its use of rhyme – if any.

HALF-RHYME   an imperfect rhyme – also known as para-rhyme, near rhyme and slant rhyme – in which the final consonants or the vowel sounds do not match. Pioneered in the 19th century by Emily Dickinson and Gerard Manley Hopkins, and made even more popular by Wilfred Owen and T S Eliot in the early 20th century,

HOMONYM   a word that is identical to another word either in sound or in spelling

HOMOPHONE   a word that is pronounced in the same way as another word but which differs in meaning and/or spelling.

HYPERBOLE

exaggeration for the sake of emphasis.

IDIOM

an everyday phrase that cannot be translated literally because its meaning does not correspond to the specific words in the phrase. There are thousands in English like – *you get up my nose, when pigs fly, she was all ears.*

IMAGERY

a rather vague critical term covering literal and metaphorical language which evoke sense impressions with reference to concrete objects – the things the writer describes.

INTERNAL RHYME

a poetic device in which two or more words in the same line rhyme.

INTERTEXTUALITY

the relationship that a text may have with another preceding and usually well-known text.

INVERSION

the reversal of the normally expected order of words. 'Normally expected' means how we might say the words in the order of normal speech; to invert the normal word order usually draws attention or foregrounds the words.

JUXTAPOSITION

two things that are placed alongside each other.

LAMENT

any poem expressing profound grief usually in the face of death.

LATINATE

Latinate diction in English means the use of words derived from Latin rather than those derived from Old English.

LITOTES	understatement – the opposite of hyperbole.
LYRIC	any fairly short poem expressing the personal mood of the speaker.
METAPHOR	the most important figure of speech in which one thing is referred to by a word normally associated with another thing, so as to suggest some common quality shared by both things. In metaphor, this similarity is directly stated, unlike in a simile where the resemblance is indirect and introduced by the words *like* or *as*. Much of our everyday language is made up of metaphor too – to say someone is *as greedy as a pig* is a simile; to say *he is a pig* is a metaphor.
MNEMONIC	a form of words or letters that helps people remember things. It is common in everyday sayings and uses some of the features of language that we associate with poetry. For example, the weather saying Red sky at night, shepherd's delight uses rhyme.
MONOLOGUE`	an extended speech uttered by one speaker.
NARRATOR	the one who tells or is assumed to be the voice of the poem.
OCTAVE or OCTET	a group of eight lines forming the first part of a sonnet.
ONOMATOPOEIA	the use of words that seem to imitate the sounds they refer to (*bang, whizz, crackle, fizz*) or any combination or words in which the sound echoes or seems to echo the sense. The adjective is onomatopoeic, so you can say that *blast* is an onomatopoeic word.

ORAL TRADITION   the passing on from one generation to another of songs, chants, poems, proverbs by word of mouth and memory.

OXYMORON   a figure of speech that combines two seemingly contradictory terms as in the everyday terms bitter-sweet and living death.

PARALLELISM   the arrangement of similarly constructed clause, sentences or lines of poetry.

PARADOX   a statement which is self-contradictory.

PATHETIC FALLACY   this is the convention that natural phenomena (usually the weather) are a reflection of the poet's or the narrator's mood. It may well involve the personification of things in nature, but does not have to. At its simplest, a writer might choose to associate very bad weather with a mood of depression and sadness.

PERSONA   the assumed identity or fictional narrator assumed by a writer.

PERSONIFICATION   a figure of speech in which animals, abstract ideas or lifeless things are referred to as if they were human. Sometimes known as personal metaphor.

PETRARCHAN   characteristic of the Italian poet Petrarch (1304 – 1374). Mainly applied to the Petrarchan sonnet which is different in its form from the Shakespearean sonnet.

PHONETIC SPELLING   a technique writers use which

involves misspelling a word in order to imitate the accent in which the word is said.

PLOSIVE
explosive. Used to describe sounds that we form by putting our lips together such as *b* and *p*.

POSTCOLONIAL LITERATURE
a term devised to describe what used to be called Commonwealth Literature (and before that Empire Writing!). The term covers a very wide range of writing from countries that were once colonies of European countries. It has come to include some writing by writers of non-white racial backgrounds whose roots or family originated in former colonies – no matter where they live now.

PUN
an expression that derives humour either through using a word that has two distinct meanings or two similar sounding words (homophones).

QUATRAIN
a verse stanza of four lines – usually rhymed.

REFRAIN
a line, or a group of lines, repeated at intervals throughout a poem – usually at regular intervals and at the end of a stanza.

RHYME
the identity of sound between syllables or paired groups of syllables usually at the end of a line of poetry.

RHYME SCHEME the pattern in which the rhymed line endings are arranged in any poem or stanza. This is normally written as a sequence of letters where each line ending in the same rhyme is given the same alphabetical letter. So a Shakespearean sonnet's rhyme scheme is ababcdcdefefgg, but the rhyme scheme of a Petrarchan sonnet is abbaabbacdecde. In other poems the rhyme scheme might be arranged to suit the poet's convenience or intentions. For example, in Blake's 'London' the first stanza rhymes abab, the second cdcd and so on.

RHYTHM   a pattern of sounds which is repeated with the stress falling on the same syllables (more or less) in each line. However, variations to the pattern, especially towards the end of the poem, often stand out and are foregrounded because they break the pattern the poet has built up through the course of the poem.

ROMANTICISM   the name given to the artistic movement that emerged in England and Germany in the 1790a and in the rest of Europe in the 1820s and beyond. It was a movement that saw great changes in literature, painting, sculpture, architecture and music and found its catalyst in the new philosophical ideas of Jean Jacques Rousseau and Thomas Paine, and in response to the French and Industrial Revolutions. Its chief emphasis was on freedom of individual self-expression, sincerity, spontaneity and originality, but it also looked to the distant past of the Middle Ages for some of its inspiration.

SATIRE   any type of writing which exposes and mocks the foolishness or evil of individuals, institutions or societies. A poem can be satiric (adjective) or you can say a poet satirizes something or somebody.

SESTET   a group of six lines forming the second half of a sonnet, following the octet.

SIBILANCE   the noticeable recurrence of *s* sounds.

SIMILE   an explicit comparison between two different things, actions or feelings, usually introduced by *like* or *as*.

SONNET   a lyric poem of 14 lines of equal length. The form originated in Italy and was made famous as a vehicle for love poetry by Petrarch and came to be adopted throughout Europe. The standard subject matter of early sonnets was romantic love, but in the 17th century John Donne used it to write religious poetry and John Milton wrote political sonnets, so it came to be used for any subject matter. The sonnet form enjoyed a revival in the Romantic period (Wordsworth, Keats and Shelley all wrote them) and continues to be widely used today. Some poets have written connected series of sonnets and these are known as sonnet cycles. Petrarchan sonnets differ slightly in their rhyme scheme from Shakespearean sonnets (see the entry above on rhyme scheme). A Petrarchan sonnet consists of two quatrains (the octet) followed by two tercets (the sestet). A Shakespearean sonnet consist of two quatrains (the octet) followed by another quatrain and a final couplet (the sestet).

STANZA   a group of verse lines forming a section of a poem and sharing the same structure in terms of the length of the lines, the rhyme scheme and the rhythm.

STYLE   any specific way of using language, which is characteristic of an author, a period, a type of poetry or a group of writers.

SYLLOGISM   a form of logical argument that draws a conclusion from two propositions. It is very characteristic of Metaphysical poetry and is exemplified in the anthology by Marvell's 'To His Coy Mistress'.

SYMBOL   anything that represents something else. A national flag symbolizes the country that uses it; symbols are heavily used in road signs. In poetry symbols can represent almost anything. Blake's 'The Sick Rose' and Armitage's 'Harmonium' are two good examples of symbols dealt with in this book.

SYNECDOCHE   a figure of speech in which a thing or person is referred to indirectly, either by naming some part of it (*hands* for manual labourers) or by naming some big thing of which it is a part (the law for police officers). As you can see from these examples, it is a common practice in speech.

TONE   a critical term meaning the mood or atmosphere of a piece of writing. It may also include the sense of the writer's attitude to the reader of the subject matter.

TURN   the English term for a sudden change in mood or line of argument, especially in line 9 of a sonnet.

VERSE   another word for poetry as opposed to prose. The use of the word 'verse' sometimes implies writing that rhymes and has a rhythm, but perhaps lacks the merit of real poetry.

VERISIMILITUDE truth-like; giving a strong sense of reality.

VERSE PARAGRAPH a group of lines of poetry forming a section of a poem, the length of the unit being determined by the sense rather than a particular stanza pattern.

VOLTA the Italian term for the 'turn' in the argument or mood of a sonnet which normally occurs in the ninth line at the start of the sestet, but sometimes in Shakespearean sonnets is delayed until the final couplet.

WIT a general term which covers the idea of intelligence, but refers in poetry more specifically to verbal ingenuity and cleverness.